Praise for *Ultimate Leadership*

"All the management advice in the world won't help you much if you can't adapt it to actual situations. That's where Russ Palmer stands out. These are smart, practical leadership principles that are tried and tested in real-world business circumstances."

—Edward Whitacre, Jr., Chairman Emeritus of AT&T, former
Chairman and CEO of AT&T and Southwest Bell

"It is very fitting that *Ultimate Leadership* is authored by Russ Palmer, the ultimate leader. It was with his guidance and friendship that I successfully transitioned from four orderly decades as a Marine to the arcane world of corporate America."

—General P.X. Kelley, USMC (Ret.),
28th Commandant of the Marine Corps

"Russ Palmer's *Ultimate Leadership* is truly the last book you'll ever need on the subject. Encapsulating scientific studies and decades of front-line experiences, Russ shows once again why he is the dean when it comes to explaining why leadership matters and how effective leadership strategies and tactics can be adapted to different settings and circumstances. Scholarly yet accessible, *Ultimate Leadership* is the ultimate statement on how leaders in business, government, and nonprofits alike can keep up with changes and conquer diverse organizational contexts."

—John J. DiIulio, Jr., Frederic Fox Leadership Professor, University of
Pennsylvania, former director, White House Office
of Faith-Based and Community Initiatives

"This book about leadership from a contextual viewpoint is nothing short of brilliant. Russ's easy-to-read book is filled with practical examples of leading from the context of a particular situation. The steps to extraordinary leadership are not hugely different, but the applications are endless. Chapter 9 about leading in a global environment is a personal favorite. Thank you, Russ, for making sense out of a very disputable subject. "

—Gerard R. Roche, Chairman of Heidrick & Struggles

"This book is refreshing proof that the essential personal traits of successful leaders are identifiable. Russ Palmer presents them in a manner providing great reading and much food for thought. "

—Gordon Bethune, Chairman, Aloha Airgroup,
former CEO, Continental Airlines

"Russ Palmer's *Ultimate Leadership* is a must-read for all those who care about the art of leadership and seek to improve their effectiveness as leaders. I was lucky enough to have Russ as a mentor during a formative part of my career, and I can say that few know more about leadership, and have the experience and wisdom to impart about it, than Russ Palmer."

—John Fry, President, Franklin & Marshall College

"Leadership is essential for all seasons, but its effective exercise depends much upon the season. In a masterful account, Russ Palmer draws on his rich store of personal experience in managing a company, running a business school, and building an enterprise to show how adaptive leadership makes the difference. For understanding what actions are required of all leaders—and how those actions must also be tailored to circumstance—*Ultimate Leadership* is the essential read."

—Michael Useem, Professor of Management and Director
of the Center for Leadership at the Wharton School,
and author of *The Go Point: When It's Time to Decide*

"Aside from being able to analyze leadership, Russ Palmer has lived a life of leadership for so many wonderful and productive years. He has managed to transfer his own life experience to paper. Truly, this is a book about leadership—not only mastering it, but having lived through all of it himself and so successfully."

—William Ruder, founder and CEO, William Ruder Incorporated

"This isn't just another book that identifies the traits of successful leaders. Russ Palmer highlights the importance of leaders understanding the context in which they operate. Successful leadership in one context may not be successful in another context. Palmer's leadership experience as CEO of the Touche Ross accounting firm and his transition to Dean of the Wharton Business School provides great insight as to understanding the importance of context."

—Robert B. Duncan, The Eli and Edythe L. Broad Dean,
The Eli Broad College of Business and The Eli Broad
Graduate School of Management, Michigan State University

ULTIMATE LEADERSHIP

ULTIMATE LEADERSHIP

Winning Execution
Strategies for
Your Situation

Russell E. Palmer

Vice President, Publisher: Tim Moore
Associate Publisher and Director of Marketing: Amy Neidlinger
Wharton Editor: Yoram (Jerry) Wind
Acquisitions Editor: Martha Cooley
Editorial Assistant: Pamela Boland
Digital Marketing Manager: Julie Phifer
Marketing Coordinator: Megan Colvin
Cover Designer: Alan Clements
Managing Editor: Gina Kanouse
Senior Project Editor: Lori Lyons
Copy Editor: Cheri Clark
Proofreader: Water Crest Publishing
Indexer: Erika Millen
Compositor: codeMantra
Manufacturing Buyer: Dan Uhrig

Wharton School Publishing offers excellent discounts on this book when ordered in quantity for
bulk purchases or special sales. For more information, please contact U.S. Corporate and
Government Sales, 1-800-382-3419, corpsales@pearsontechgroup.com. For sales outside the
U.S., please contact International Sales at international@pearsoned.com.

Printed in the United States of America

First Printing January 2008

ISBN-10: 0-13-193386-8
ISBN-13: 978-0-13-193386-6

Pearson Education LTD.
Pearson Education Australia PTY, Limited.
Pearson Education Singapore, Pte. Ltd.
Pearson Education North Asia, Ltd.
Pearson Education Canada, Ltd.
Pearson Educatión de Mexico, S.A. de C.V.
Pearson Education—Japan
Pearson Education Malaysia, Pte. Ltd.

Library of Congress Cataloging-in-Publication Data

Palmer, Russell E.
  Ultimate leadership : winning execution strategies for your situation / Russell Palmer.
    p. cm.
  ISBN 0-13-193386-8 (hardback : alk. paper)
  1. Leadership. I. Title.
  HD57.7.P349 2007
  658.4'092--dc22
                              2007026911

To
My Wife Wendy

The Kids
Brad ✦ *Steve* ✦ *Russell* ✦ *Karen*

The Grandkids
Amelia ✦ *Isabella* ✦ *Jackson* ✦ *Kate* ✦ *Kayleigh*
Lizzie ✦ *Natalie* ✦ *Sophia* ✦ *Teddy*

CONTENTS

FOREWORD

I first came to know Russell Palmer in 1999. He had been serving on the board of directors of GTE when the company merged with Bell Atlantic to form Verizon Communications, where he continued serving on the Verizon Board. From the beginning I was impressed with Russ' ability to add valuable insights and guidance to our Board, our management, and to me personally. His contributions went much further than his broad knowledge of markets, financials matters, and corporate governance. Russ has developed a keen understanding of the role of leadership in building successful organizations.

In this book, Russ has distilled knowledge and wisdom about leadership that he acquired in his years as Managing Director of Touche Ross, Dean of the Wharton School of Business at the University of Pennsylvania, and now Chairman and Chief Executive of his own firm, The Palmer Group. What particularly distinguishes his book is its focus on the different situations or "contexts" in which leaders must act and the articulation of a pragmatic set of principles to apply in practicing effective leadership. Russ describes a range of typical contexts and provides guidance for leaders to develop their own effective leadership style. There are many real examples, both positive and negative, to demonstrate how these principles work in the real world.

As a leader himself, Russ was successful in each of the three organizational contexts he led. I have no doubt that his success was due in no small part to his skill in working with his people, as was obvious from his participation on our board of directors. In the book he takes a conversational tone that communicates a feeling of an experienced leader mentoring leaders and would-be leaders.

Russ retired from the Verizon Board in 2005, and since then I have missed his wise counsel. I wish him well in his new role as an author.

Ivan Seidenberg
Chairman and Chief Executive Officer
Verizon Communications, Inc.

PREFACE

This is a book about an aspect of leadership that leaders, or aspiring leaders, need to understand but is too often overlooked. It is what I call "context."

My central premise is that the principles of leadership can be effective in a wide variety of situations, but they often need to be applied in a very different manner depending on the circumstances and the constituent groups involved. The principles of leadership and this context-driven approach to leadership form the book's two basic themes. In other words, this book argues that for leaders to be effective—whether they head a multimillion-dollar corporation with thousands of employees or a small not-for-profit organization with half a dozen volunteers—it is important that they focus not just on the principles of successful leadership, but also on the context in which the principles are applied. Understanding the context enables leaders to execute effectively.

Though the concept of context sounds simple, in fact it has many dimensions, and I describe various contexts and the leadership styles that work in each. If you don't find the specific context in which you operate, you should not assume that the book has nothing to say to you. Each of the contexts I describe can apply to related organizations and industries. I contend that there is no industry or organization that is exempt from the realities of leadership that I explore in this book. The leader who understands the demands of context is well-armed for the future no matter what it may bring.

There is another context that leaders need to be aware of. In today's world, leaders are not infrequently called upon to serve in boards of industry associations, government policy advisory commissions, and other outside organizations that can require quite different leadership styles from what they are used to in the home office. I point out the pitfalls that await successful leaders when they are called upon to work outside their own organizations. These outside contexts can be quite different, and success or failure can often depend on modifying leadership styles to suit a different context.

What qualifications do I bring to an understanding of leadership? In my professional lifetime, I have had the good fortune to have had three very different successful leadership careers. The first was in the world of accounting, where I was named managing partner of Touche Ross, now Deloitte and Touche, at the age of 37. Next, during the turbulent 1980s, I became the Dean of the Wharton School of the University of Pennsylvania and served in that post for seven years. I also taught the leadership course to MBA students. Finally, since 1990, I have led The Palmer Group, a private investment firm, with the goal of "having fun and doing something meaningful." All of our investments to date have been successful.

Jack Welch, the legendary former CEO of General Electric, once told me that it is remarkable for one individual to combine three very different major careers during a professional lifespan. The advantage for me is that each of these careers has taught me a lot about the demands of leadership in different contexts.

An experience I had in my last year at Wharton led indirectly to my decision to write this book. A contingent from a very prestigious business school came to visit me. They told me they were setting up a school of leadership. These people knew that I had taught a leadership course at Wharton, and that I was going to be leaving in a few months. They visited me to get some ideas about teaching leadership, but I am sure the underlying thought was whether I might be interested in being associated with this new school.

I asked what they were trying to do in their school of leadership, and they looked at me as though this was not a particularly insightful question. Obviously, a leadership school was meant "to produce outstanding leaders." "That is a noble goal," I said. "I assume you will have a tracking system to see how effective the new school will be in doing that." They said they hadn't particularly addressed that problem, though it was certainly something to think about.

Next, I asked them to tell me the background for students to be admitted to this new school. This was an area they had briefly covered in their overview of the school. They said that students would be admitted from schools throughout the university. The students would submit an application, and the admissions office would look at grades and such to decide whether they could get in, but anyone who applied would probably be admitted. When I asked how they would determine the leadership potential of the students they were planning to admit, they said they did not contemplate doing that. The faculty, in setting up the school, had been adamant that they did not want to discriminate against those who wanted to join the school by trying to sort them according to their leadership potential. They thought the school should just make everyone better leaders than they would otherwise be.

"So how will you reconcile those two goals?" I asked. "How will you join the principle you just mentioned—of admitting anyone who applies and improving their leadership ability—with the other goal of developing outstanding leaders, and perhaps tracking how they did in the future?" The reply was that this too was a question that needed to be addressed.

The fact is that I had already decided not to go to another academic setting. But even if I had decided to stay in academia, this certainly would not have been an opportunity I would have pursued. It seemed to me that their idea of leadership was not based on the hard realities of the competitive marketplace that I had experienced at Touche Ross or the special demands on the Dean of the Wharton School.

The experience kept nagging me as I prepared to leave Wharton and embark on my third career as a corporate investor. I saw the disconnect between their understanding of leadership and mine. I believed that I had enough experience as a leader and teacher to put it all down in a systematic form that would help today's leaders and tomorrow's. I was helped immeasurably by the truly outstanding group of leaders who contributed to the book. It's amazing how similar our ideas about leadership are. This book is the result.

ABOUT THE AUTHOR

Russell E. Palmer is the owner and Chairman and Chief Executive Officer of The Palmer Group, a corporate investment firm located in Philadelphia, Pennsylvania. Before founding his own firm, he served as Dean of the Wharton School for seven years and prior to that he served for ten years as Managing Partner and CEO of Touche Ross & Co. (now Deloitte & Touche), an accounting and consulting firm. He became CEO of Touche Ross at age 37, the youngest person ever to attain that position in what is now the "Big Four" accounting firms.

After 27 years in the accounting and consulting profession, Mr. Palmer became Dean of the Wharton School. As the tenth Dean, and the first to come from the private sector, he shared his management experience with MBA students in a leadership course that he developed. He was instrumental in attracting more than 100 new faculty members to the School, building a new executive education program and complex and raising more than $125 million for the School. When he retired, the school was consistently ranked number one in undergraduate business education and in the top three MBA graduate programs.

In his current career with The Palmer Group, he has acquired more than thirty companies with the majority being in the educational field. All of these acquisitions have been successful investments, with the latest divestiture being a proprietary school group that was sold for $120 million.

Active in the outside business community, Mr. Palmer has served on 12 New York Stock Exchange boards, including Honeywell International, Inc., Verizon Communications, Inc.,

The May Department Stores Company, The Goodyear Tire & Rubber Company, and Bethlehem Steel Corporation. He is a Trustee Emeritus of the University of Pennsylvania, a Trustee of the National Constitution Center, and a Member of the Smithsonian National Board.

Mr. Palmer graduated with a Bachelor of Arts degree, cum laude, from Michigan State University, and has received several honorary degrees. He has written and lectured extensively. His articles and essays have appeared in *Business Week*, the *New York Times*, the *Journal of Accountancy*, and other publications.

LIST OF CONTRIBUTORS

Gordon Bethune, Chairman, Aloha Airgroup (parent of Aloha Airlines); former CEO, Continental Airlines

Larry Bossidy, former CEO, Honeywell; author

Virginia Clark, director of external affairs, Smithsonian Institution

David M. Cote, CEO and Chairman, Honeywell

John J. DiIulio, Jr., professor at the University of Pennsylvania; Jesuit leadership expert; head of President Bush's Office of Faith-Based and Community Initiative

Tom Ehrlich, former provost of the University of Pennsylvania; former president of Indiana University; former dean of Stanford Law School

Marsha Evans, former president of the Red Cross and the Girl Scouts; Admiral of the U.S. Navy

Gen. P.X. Kelley, former commandant, Marine Corps

Yotaro (Tony) Kobayashi, Chairman, Fuji Xerox

John R. McKernan, former governor of Maine; Chairman of Education Management Corp.

David Reibstein, professor of marketing at the Wharton School; former vice dean, Wharton graduate division

Uriel Reichman, president and founder of The Interdisciplinary Center in Herzliya, Israel

Gen. Eric K. Shinseki, former Army Chief of Staff

Michael Useem, professor of management at the Wharton School; director, Center for Leadership and Change Management

Jacob Wallenberg, Chairman of the Board, Investor, SEB Skandinaviska Enskilda Banken, and W Capital Management

Yoram (Jerry) Wind, professor of marketing at the Wharton School; director, SEI Center for Advanced Studies in Management

ACKNOWLEDGMENTS

When I started to write this book, I didn't know how many people it was going to take to help me complete it, but I have been blessed with strong support; and actually that has been one of the joys of putting this all together because I was able to work with a group of people whom I know and respect.

Mukul Pandya is the Executive Director/Editor-in-Chief of Knowledge@Wharton. His help in this book was immeasurable. He did research, he put together material, he did a significant number of the interviews from contributors, and he deciphered some of my tapes to make them sound better than when I transcribed them. What a great person to work with.

Herb Addison was another joy to work with as the editor of the book. My regard for him grew as I worked with him, and in addition, when I would mention to people associated with the publishing trade that I was working with him, they were extremely impressed and said, "You're working with Herb Addison, who was a former executive editor at Oxford Press and now does freelance work." I hadn't known I was working with such a well-known person.

The contributors were just great. They gave a considerable amount of their time to the interviews, and it was especially meaningful to me that not only were they willing to contribute but for some time I have been able to count each of them as my friend.

Jerry Wind and Mike Useem not only were contributors but also agreed to read the book in draft form. Their insight and comments were very helpful in making some key changes.

I am grateful to all of my colleagues who agreed to devote some time to talk about my days from Touche Ross or the Wharton School or my current business. These included John Keydel, Tom Presby, Carl Griffin, Gerard Francois, Bill Brooks, Dave Reibstein, and others.

I am especially indebted to my ever faithful Jean Drake, my assistant, who may have been thinking when we took on this project that we have enough to do around here already without writing a book. She kept all the multi-drafts sorted out, and she even had to sort me out a few times.

And of course my wonderful wife, Wendy, was supportive and helpful through the entire process.

So, thanks so much. I've done my best, and I hope it is a worthy reflection of the outstanding efforts you all contributed.

Unlocking the Secrets of Successful Leadership

Chapter 1

LEADERSHIP PRINCIPLES: THE BASIS OF SUCCESSFUL LEADERSHIP

There is no single style of leadership that works. But there are basic principles of leadership that all effective leaders apply regardless of their personal style of leadership. This book is about those principles.

But the book is also about the greatest mistake that a leader can make. That is to fail to understand how important it is to adapt these principles to the particular context in which the leader is operating. What works in the corner office of the leader's own organization can be a disaster when applied mindlessly in other contexts. What do I mean by context?

I mean not only the context of the organizations that leaders lead but also the other environments in which they often operate. Here is an example. Larry Bossidy, former CEO of Honeywell International, was asked how he would react if he were chairing a business round-table of other CEOs charged with advising the government on business policy. He replied:

> What is good for the goose isn't always good for the gander. In other words, if you have CEOs around the table, depending on the business they operate, they might take relatively pedestrian positions that benefit their own companies. You can't blame them for that. I've done this, as a matter of fact. However, you might say something like, "This business round-table has as one of its goals to influence legislation. And if the legislation we are

considering goes the way it's being proposed, it will certainly have an effect on business. It may not have an effect on your business, or it may have a slightly positive effect on your business. But in the general interest of the round-table, it will have an overall detrimental effect." So you appeal to their sense of logic and decency. At the end of the day, you don't automatically command all those votes unanimously, but you still make a recommendation for what should be done for the majority of those on the round-table.

Bossidy knew that he could not simply issue an order as he might at his own company—and in fact, he probably did not order people even at Honeywell unless he absolutely had to do so. He needed to be sensitive to the egos of other CEOs and to find a common chord of understanding around which they could come together.

So the underlying theme of this book is that to be successful, leaders must understand and apply the principles of leadership and at the same time shape the application of the principles to the differing contexts in which they find themselves. Put more simply, if a leader combines leadership principles with an understanding of context, there will be effective execution. Though the idea seems obvious, I have seen able leaders fail to grasp this reality and find themselves unable to lead organizations that are in desperate need of effective leadership.

Here's an example from my own experience. Soon after I became Dean of the Wharton School, we developed a program called the Plan for Pre-eminence (about which I will say more in another chapter). Its goal was to make Wharton the top business school in the U.S., and it had many various elements, including, for instance, recruiting top faculty members from leading institutions around the country (eventually we recruited more than 100 faculty members in seven years). The plan had many other facets, including revamping the MBA curriculum, pushing forward aggressively on fundraising, transforming our Executive Education programs, and building new facilities, along with other initiatives. For the plan to succeed, we needed every constituency at the school—faculty, staff, students, alumni, and so on—to pull together to achieve it.

Getting students to support the plan was not as easy as it might sound. Reflect for a moment, if you will, upon the circumstances of someone who decides to interrupt a career to get an MBA degree. Most of the students had taken two years off from their careers and had deferred earning a salary to get the degree, and they were paying a high tuition rate to boot. The last thing on their minds was a new plan that some new dean had introduced—and they were not exactly pleased at the prospect of interrupting their busy study and job-interview schedule to support it. They had their own goals—getting a good degree, and a good job making money—and they were at Wharton to attain those objectives. Why should the Plan for Pre-eminence matter to them?

We had to convince the students as to why the plan mattered, and how it served their present and future interests. I met regularly with students to discuss the plan, and in our conversations I would say something along these lines: "How important is the reputation of the school you attend to your career? If you go to Harvard, or Stanford, or Wharton, is that better for you than going to a school whose reputation is not quite as strong? For the rest of your life, people are going to ask you where you went to school. They will make initial judgments about you based on whether you went to a top school or a mediocre one. If we can make Wharton the top business school, it will be an advantage for a lifetime for every one of you and everyone who has graduated from here."

Gradually, after countless conversations, the message sank in that Wharton's reputation was as crucial to the students' future as many of the concepts they were learning in class. They understood how important it was to support the Plan for Pre-eminence, and how they would benefit from its success. Their goals and the goals of the institution were joined. We aligned our objectives. The students' attitude changed, they threw their weight behind the plan, and it became easier to accomplish the school's strategic goals.

This is just one example of how change can be brought about. Leadership involves many tasks—but one of the most important ones is to cause change. This is one of the most difficult things to do in any organization—because the beliefs, habits, processes, and environment have been solidified over a long period. In general, people don't mind change as long as it does not affect them. But if a change is disruptive of their activities or their lives or their normal patterns, people often dislike that—and they resist change vehemently and vocally.

How can leaders bring about change? In part, they do it by gaining the commitment of their constituents. Leaders convince their constituents to support plans for change because it benefits them to do so. In other words, employees must be convinced that when they back an initiative for change, it will benefit them tangibly and concretely—in terms of their promotion, or their bonus, or their salary—even if these things don't happen right away. They are not going to support a plan for change just because the leader happens to think it is a good idea. Wise leaders also don't use threats—"Either you do what I say or you're fired." The negative, fear-oriented approach never achieves as much over the long term as a consensus-building, enthusiastic approach to transforming an organization. (One CEO often told his subordinates that he wanted all of them to be fired with enthusiasm, or they would be fired with enthusiasm.)

When you, as a leader, are trying to bring about change in an environment that isn't in a catastrophic situation, the first thing to realize is that trying to change an organization is like trying to tear down a brick wall without tools. If you try to do it all at once, you will end up with aching arms and perhaps bloody knuckles— but the wall will still stand. The right approach is to wait for a brick to loosen, and then push it over to the other side. Then you go for the next brick. You will find that some things can be changed faster at certain times due to existing circumstances than other things can. To succeed as a leader, you need to seize the opportunities you find to change those things—rather than working twice as hard on changing something that isn't yet ready for change.

If you focus on things that are very difficult to change, you may just end up causing disruption and lose momentum or cause a revolution. You can't be too far in front of the troops. You may know what is likely to happen and what has to be done, but if you are too far ahead of the ranks, you are in trouble. You have to move the group along so that its members generally agree with what is happening. On the other hand, the leader can use a situation in which real danger is present to accomplish a great deal in a short time. We will discuss these issues with more examples later in this book.

Who Should Read the Book?

I have written this book for anyone who is a leader or an aspiring leader. The principles I describe will work in a wide variety of organizations. These include manufacturing companies, high-tech companies, foundations, arts organizations, government, the military, partnerships, service organizations, financial institutions, and educational organizations, among others.

In the book, I describe various contexts that can be found in today's organizations, and I explain the kinds of leadership styles that work best in each. But it would be a mistake for readers to assume that because there might be no chapter on an organization that exactly matches the context of their own organization that the book has no relevance to them. Many of the contexts described in the chapters are very close to a wide range of similar organizations, and the leadership styles that work in them are essentially the same. I argue that there are no industries or organizations that are so different from those in this book that they are exempt from the tools I present for leadership in the 21st century.

The key concepts in the book are strengthened by the voices of a remarkable set of leaders that are woven into the text. They were invited to tell us about their ideas and experience of leadership, and they include corporate leaders such as Larry Bossidy, the former CEO of Honeywell, whom we have just heard from, as well as its current CEO and chairman, David M. Cote. You will also hear from Tony Kobayashi, the chairman of Fuji Xerox; Gen. P.X. Kelley, former commandant of the Marine Corps.; Gen. Eric K. Shinseki, who headed the Joint Chiefs of Staff and led the U.S. military effort to bring peace to Bosnia; Jock McKernan, former governor of Maine, who is now Chairman of Education Management Corp. in Pittsburgh; Marty Evans, a former Naval officer who was the highest ranking woman in the Navy at that time and who later headed the Red Cross; John DiIulio, a professor at the University of Pennsylvania who once headed President George W. Bush's Faith-Based and Community Initiatives and is a Jesuit leadership expert; Tom Ehrlich, former provost of the University of Pennsylvania, former president of Indiana University, and also former dean of Stanford Law School; Uriel Reichman, who once fought as an officer in the Israeli army and later was the founder and president of The Interdisciplinary Center in Herzliya, Israel; Jacob Wallenberg, who belongs to Sweden's well-known banking family and now is chairman of the board of Investor, SEB Skandinaviska Enskilda Banken and W Capital Management; and Virginia Clark, head of external affairs for the Smithsonian Museum. In addition, you will hear from several leaders with whom I worked—or continue to work—at Touche Ross, the Wharton School, and The Palmer Group. All these individuals present their own perspectives on leadership—but these serve a common purpose: To help you get a richer and deeper appreciation of the principles and context of leadership.

In this chapter, I will briefly describe the principles that I believe are essential to successful leadership. In subsequent chapters, I will describe the many contexts in which leaders are likely to find themselves and explain how to adapt the basic principles to these differing contexts.

The Basic Principles of Successful Leadership

Regardless of the kind of organization, a leader must master and apply these principles:

- A leader at all times must embody a personal integrity, which is the foundation of leadership. Followers want to believe that their leader is unshakably fair in public and in private.
- A leader applies basically the same principles of leadership regardless of context, but the style of execution is very different in different contexts. That is, execution in leadership is to a great extent about context.
- In normal times, a leader should make faster progress taking opportunities that are ready for change rather than trying to take on areas that the leader knows will be more resisted. Later these resistance areas could be more conducive to change.
- In times of crisis, a leader must step out ahead of the followers and make the difficult decisions without consensus and at times even without adequate explanation in order to resolve the threat to the organization.
- A leader's ultimate goal is to release the human potential of the followers. This will benefit not only the followers but also the overall organization.
- In today's global marketplace, leaders need to foster innovation at all levels of the organization, and that means listening to workers and giving them ample latitude to experiment, make mistakes, and seek new products and services that will compete in a constantly changing competitive landscape.
- A leader mobilizes followers by finding out their goals, desires, wants, and needs, and makes them believe that the

leader is truly trying to help them achieve these aspirations. At the same time, in order to achieve the goals of the organization, the leader must bridge the individual goals of the followers and the overall goals that are incorporated in, for example, a strategic plan.

- A leader's most important and essential attribute is good judgment. This is innate and really can't be taught, although it can be matured with experience.

- A leader must build confidence among the followers. Like teachers, a leader must communicate high expectations and then ensure that followers develop confidence that they can meet those expectations. They can who think they can.

- A leader must give considerable thought and careful execution to the whole area of rational and intangible rewards in relation to motivation of followers. For example, it is critical to the execution of a strategic plan that the compensation system be tied to the plan and not exclusively to earnings per share or the budget.

- A leader can't get too far out in front of the troops in leading without risking failure to achieve the leader's goals. A leader will always be ahead in thinking, but the group must be brought along so that members understand what is happening and why—or the leader may be faced with a disconnect between the leader's goals and those that the members are willing to accept.

- A leader must communicate the leader's goals to the entire organization—ideally in person, but at least in writing in his or her own words—since communication is crucial to an effective organization.

- A leader serves as a symbol and is perceived by followers to be on a different plane from the rest of the organization. Thus, the leader is constrained in what behavior is appropriate and not appropriate. He or she can only go so far in being "one of the boys."

- Leadership is the main differentiator in performance in most environments. People think that formulas, slick marketing, being first, the latest management tool, programs such as Six Sigma, and so on are the key differentiators in an organization. These other areas matter, but leadership alone is the key differentiator between organizations that succeed and those that fail.

I will return to these principles throughout the book as I explain how context affects the way they are applied.

The Plan of the Book

The book is organized according to the contexts that leaders are most likely to encounter. It is not meant to be exhaustive—and thereby risk being exhausting—but rather to provide models that can help you apply the principles of leadership in contexts that I do not specifically cover.

The first two chapters are a general introduction to the fundamentals of leadership. The central theme of Chapter 2, "The Many Contexts of Leadership," is that leaders are often not aware that the different contexts in which they operate can require them to adapt their leadership style in order to be successful. I list some of the more important contexts that I develop more completely in later chapters.

Chapters 3 through 9, grouped under the title, "Mastering the Contexts of Leadership," are the heart of the book and describe the contexts that all leaders should be aware of to be successful. They begin with Chapter 3, "The Top-Down Organization: Learning That It's Not So Simple." Even a strong leader in a typical hierarchical organization can soon find out that dealing with outside organizations often requires a more collaborative style than the direct organizational style that works at the home office. In this chapter, and in all of the chapters in "Mastering the Contexts of Leadership," I weave in the principles of leadership that I have described above as appropriate to the context.

Chapter 4, "The Organization of Peers: Leading Your Equals," takes you into the ambiguous world of dealing with peers. You will perhaps find no challenge that is more difficult than working with other leaders to achieve some common purpose. I suggest a number of ways that you can meet this challenge.

I believe that though effective leadership is always important to the success of an organization, it is absolutely critical in times of crisis. In Chapter 5, "The Organization in Crisis: Turning Danger into Opportunity," I argue that leaders need to look at crises as opportunities. Yes, a crisis is a danger, but it also can provide the platform for fundamental organization transformation into a vibrant new player in whatever environment you happen to be operating.

It is not enough to realize the need for change in your organization. You must often face the opposition of the organization's culture that may view change as a threat. In Chapter 6, "When Organizations Change: Transforming the Culture," I describe the two major kinds of change—change within a single organization and the change that occurs when two different organizations merge—and explain ways that you can reassure balky workers that they have more to fear from not changing than from changing to meet a changed world.

There are special challenges for entrepreneurial leaders, and in Chapter 7, "The Entrepreneurial Organization: Sharing Your Vision with Others," I make the point that entrepreneurs have a unique position: They are alone. They may have investors, advisors, and so forth, but they are the decision makers, and usually make decisions very quickly. This makes it possible for entrepreneurs to execute very fast. That is why entrepreneurial environments provide fertile ground for leadership. But the risk is that entrepreneurs may try to do it all rather than develop a group of trusted associates who can share the burden of decision making.

Leaders outside of the academic world often consider it an ivory tower with nothing to teach those in the "real world." I believe this to be a great mistake, and in Chapter 8, "The Academic

Organization: Learning from the Wharton Experience," I describe—partly from my own experience—how academic leaders often face the same kinds of challenges as other leaders. Their responses hold valuable lessons for those outside the academic world.

Even in your own organization, there are different contexts. In Chapter 9, "National Cultures and Context: Leading in a Global Environment," I describe how leaders must understand the special place that culture and social norms occupy in a global organization. Leadership styles that work well in some cultures may be perceived as handicaps in others.

Having explored the different contexts in which leaders may be required to exercise leadership principles, in Chapter 10, "The Heart of Leadership: Motivating Workers," I return to describe possibly the most important attribute every leader must have: the ability to motivate his or her constituents. Finally, in Chapter 11, "Putting It Altogether," I return to the principles of leadership and describe how they can differ in application depending on different contexts.

Leadership Versus Management

I conclude this chapter by asking an important question in a book on leadership: Is there a difference between management and leadership? Again, let us hear from Larry Bossidy, with whom I agree:

> Yes there is. Management is the art of getting things done by using administrative skills to organize, plan, and execute. Leadership is all that, but it is also more motivational, more visionary, and it requires more in terms of personal attributes of the leader. In other words, management is administration, while leadership is vision, strategy, and motivation. Each requires a different set of attributes.

This does not mean that a manager cannot aspire to be a successful leader. In fact, most leaders began as managers somewhere in the organization. They were leaders then also, but they just didn't have the platform. But to become an effective leader you have to transcend the requirements of management and demonstrate the attributes of a true leader.

It is the purpose of this book to help you do just that. I should clarify that my purpose is not to offer tools of the "one-minute manager" variety, but to build on the skills you already have and help you mature them by making you aware of how to use the principles of leadership in different contexts.

Summary

- There are basic principles of leadership that you must master in order to be effective in your own organization.
- You will succeed in the larger task of leadership only if you adapt the basic principles of leadership to the varied contexts in which you will find yourself.

Chapter 2

THE MANY CONTEXTS OF LEADERSHIP

One of the biggest mistakes a leader can make is to fail to understand that what works in the leader's own organization can be very wrong in other contexts that may be a part of the leader's wider responsibilities. I have seen leaders who were brilliant in shaping their own organizations fail utterly when they found themselves in leadership roles in very different kinds of organizations.

Why that happens will be our theme in this chapter. I describe a number of different leadership contexts and briefly explore the special challenges facing their leaders. Each of the contexts requires a different approach to leadership, and I suggest what styles work best in each case. I again point out that the list is not meant to be an exhaustive survey of every possible context. Rather, I expect that most readers will recognize what kind of organization they are in among those I discuss. Just keep in mind that no matter what leadership style works best in your organization, it might not work at all if you find yourself, for whatever reason, either temporarily or permanently in one of the other kinds of organizations I describe.

Command-and-Control Organizations

Is there still such a thing as command-and-control leadership? Probably not in the purest sense of the term. But there are industries in which the board holds the top leader's feet to the fire and expects results—or else. Such leaders are accustomed to wielding great power. Authority devolves from the top down, and the organization generally marches in lock step. Industries that tend to have this mode of operation include automotive, defense, and construction. But there are other industries and organizations where this leadership style prevails, and you should easily know if you are in one yourself.

In my experience, leaders nurtured in command-and-control organizations often are the ones who find it most difficult to adapt to organizational contexts that require a more collegial approach. This is especially true of leaders in industry who move to positions in academia, government, partnership firms, or, for that matter, any organization that needs a collegial approach as opposed to a "do it and do it now" mentality.

In today's global economy, marked as it is by growing trends like outsourcing and offshoring, command-and-control organizations often appear as vestiges of the old military-industrial complex and its bureaucratic leadership styles. In most business organizations today, hierarchies are being flattened; persuasion rather than command is the dominant form of communication; and authority is ambiguous—it is often exercised laterally rather than in top-down fashion. It is also true, however, that old habits die hard, and in some situations nothing but a top-down approach to leadership will work in making things happen.

The chapter on top-down leadership that follows offers examples of cases in which top-down leadership worked well, and also a few possible pitfalls. Companies like GE and Home Depot, for example, have recruited former military officers and used their services to obtain strong business results. A major pitfall of this style of leadership, however, is that the leader sometimes tends to become increasingly arrogant, isolated, and even alienated from his or her constituents. And when that happens, as the ancient Greek dramatists knew so well, Hubris against the gods is often followed by the retribution of Nemesis.

Partnerships of Peers

Leading an organization of partners requires great skill and tact. In theory, everyone is equal in a partnership, but effective functioning requires that someone be appointed first among equals. The challenge facing this kind of leader, who has some idea of what needs to be done to meet changing conditions, is how to communicate with the others. The leader's task is to engage partners in a way that brings them onboard in the process of change. Such organizations include Big Four accounting firms, management consulting firms, law firms, physicians' organizations, and organizations involving knowledge workers.

This is an organizational context where my own personal experience has taught me much about leadership. At Touche Ross, now Deloitte and Touche, as well as the Wharton School, the prevailing organizational culture emphasized peer-to-peer leadership rather than the top-down variety. As I will show in detail in later chapters, at Touche Ross successful leadership entailed uniting the partners around a common vision of helping build an innovative firm, and at Wharton as the dean I had to rally the faculty and other constituents around a plan for preeminence. Neither of these efforts would have succeeded if I had used an autocratic approach.

Anyone who leads an organization like this has an advantage when confronted by the challenges of other contexts that require a collegial approach.

Entrepreneurial Organizations

Among all the kinds of leaders, entrepreneurs are unique. They are alone. Of course, they work with investors and advisors, but they are the ultimate decision makers. This allows them to make decisions quickly and to execute rapidly. Entrepreneurial contexts are a fertile ground for leadership. But the challenge entrepreneurial leaders face is knitting together the investors, advisors, customers, vendors, and others, with their vision. That is a matter of negotiation. It is the price the entrepreneur must pay.

When entrepreneurs find themselves in other contexts, they need to restrain their natural instinct to take charge and make decisions if collegial leadership is required.

After leaving the Wharton School, I have spent most my time building The Palmer Group, which invests in entrepreneurial ventures. As such, I have had lots of dealings with entrepreneurial leaders—and I will share with you both the lessons I've learned and the mistakes I've made, which I hope you will avoid. You will read more about this in Chapter 7, "The Entrepreneurial Organization: Sharing Your Vision with Others," but I would say one of the most important lessons entrepreneurial leaders need to learn is to work with the right partners. Have lots of due diligence about whom you are working with—and you will find that the effort is worth it. An important mistake to avoid is waiting too long to make money. Your goal as an entrepreneur should be to try to generate a profit as soon as is reasonably possible.

The Academic World

It may be a cliché to say that leading a faculty of independent-minded professors is like herding cats. But it's not far from the truth. Professors can usually decide what research to pursue and how to teach their courses, and most of them generally believe that they have no boss. This makes the role of an academic administrator, such as a dean or college president, especially challenging. It's one of the roles in which I served, and I can attest to how careful an academic administrator needs to be to accomplish anything. If there is a need for significant change, the challenge is even more difficult.

Nevertheless, the lessons a successful dean or college president learns on the job can be applied in a number of other contexts.

Business Round-Tables and Other Peer Groups

The more successful top executives become, the more in demand they are likely to be to serve on round-tables, boards of industry associations, government commissions, and the like. Here they have to work with equally accomplished executives from other organizations who are not about to sit back and let someone else take charge. However, someone is usually designated to be the chair, and to get anything done the chair has to tactfully lead these contending egos to agreement on agenda items.

Executives who have served as chairs on effective boards of peers have been through a trial by fire that can temper and deepen their leadership skills.

Nonprofits

Leaders in nonprofit contexts face a discipline not unlike that of the bottom line that leaders in the business world face. They have to balance what they spend with what they take in. Examples of nonprofits include grant-making foundations, think tanks, arts organizations, and charities. Leaders in these organizations often have to spend much of their time fundraising, and that generally requires a very different style of leadership from the corporate world. Even when there is no need for fundraising—for example, in a well-endowed foundation—the top executive needs to work cooperatively with a board of governors that is likely to have definite ideas about the foundation's mission and agenda. Nonprofit organizations often are dependent on volunteers who don't view themselves as employees and often act as free agents. Moreover, while I don't mean to generalize, volunteers can sometimes have a lot of opinions that are not based on facts. All this tends to make managing a nonprofit a difficult challenge for the leader.

The Military

Leadership style in the military is similar to that in command-and-control organizations. An order is an order. An obvious difference, however, is that in the military, lives are at stake. And in the U.S. military, tactical decision making has been pushed down the hierarchy to combat leaders who must respond to moment-to-moment changes on the battlefield. The best top military leaders understand that they must set broad strategic goals that are clear and step back and let those on the line implement the goals using their best judgment. On the other hand, I have often been struck by the fact that top military leaders have a surprising amount of political skill and collegial ability when these are necessary. Perhaps these skills are developed as part of a need to be successful in promotion and dealing with large numbers of superiors.

Military leaders often make a smooth transition to positions of leadership in industry and other contexts.

Government

Leadership in government differs from almost every other kind of context because, in the final analysis, everyone is your boss. You have been hired, or elected, to carry out the will of the people. Broadly speaking, there are two kinds of government leaders: those who hold elective office and those who head government departments, agencies, commissions, and other nonelective governmental organizations. In both cases, the leadership role can be ambiguous. That is because both types of leaders are visible to the public at large. What they do is scrutinized by the public and the media, and they can be called to account in a public forum when things go wrong.

Leaders who move from government to the private sector may not err on the side of being too assertive, but they may err on the side of being too cautious and bureaucratic.

The Operating Room

The scene in an operating room is one of complete autocracy. The surgeon is in charge and no one questions his or her orders. When the surgeon asks for a certain kind of scalpel, none of those attending the operation debates whether it is the correct instrument. It is perhaps one of the purest forms of a command-and-control context.

I include this context to remind you that it is unlikely that you will actually have the authority of a surgeon in other contexts. It works only if you are a surgeon yourself.

Organizations in Crisis

When an organization is in crisis, the collegial leadership rule book gets thrown out. There is a need for leadership to become very concise. There is not a lot of time to deliberate over and discuss decisions. The leader has to step forward and personally take charge. The leader still requires a type of strategic plan, but there is no time for collegiality and little room for delegation. A crisis calls for execution—rapid execution—while being calm under fire. But a crisis also can be turned into an opportunity. It can be very revealing, especially about one's peers. You never know fully about people around you until you have seen them under fire. It can be a bonding experience.

Once the crisis has passed, the leader has to know when to relax the grip on the reins and allow authority to flow down the hierarchy, both for the long-term health of the organization and to develop its future leaders.

Summary

- It is crucial to your success as a leader to understand that effective leadership styles need to vary with the context and to adapt your style to the context of your own organization.

- Successful leaders can fail to understand that the leadership style that works in their own organizations can be very wrong in other leadership roles in which they may find themselves. Recognizing this reality can help you make the transition to a different leadership style when that is necessary in a new context.
- This chapter presents you with a number of different leadership contexts and describes the style that works best in each.

Mastering the Contexts of Leadership

Chapters 3 through 9 describe various contexts that require leaders to adopt varying leadership styles that will be most effective within each. I tell what kinds of styles leaders should adopt so that they will connect with their workers and bring them onboard in a cooperative effort to move forward and achieve strategic objectives.

Chapter 3

THE TOP-DOWN ORGANIZATION: LEARNING THAT IT'S NOT SO SIMPLE

This chapter explores a range of organizational contexts that I believe are vital to understand if leaders are to succeed. Each of the chapters presents a different kind of context and describes how things get done in that context and the leadership style that will be most effective in it. In Chapter 1, "Leadership Principles: The Basis of Successful Leadership," I presented a set of management principles that I believe apply to every context I discuss in the book. There are occasions in these context chapters that I mention one or more of these principles that are especially relevant to my discussion. I caution you not to conclude that this is the only principle that applies. The fact is, they all apply in each context I discuss.

Every leadership context has its potential pitfalls, and effective leadership requires avoiding them. I point out a number of these so that you can become aware of potential hazards on the leadership road ahead.

As a leader in one context, you may find yourself operating in other contexts that differ significantly as a part of your responsibilities. Sometimes the leadership style appropriate to your present job can work in other contexts, and sometimes it can be disastrously wrong. I describe both situations.

Context: The Top-Down Organization

Even as many organizations are striving for a collegial style of management, there are still firms and organizations that are run essentially from the top down. Here are some examples based on my experience: Automakers, defense contractors, airlines, and construction firms have typically had strong "do it and do it now" leaders. Outside of industries, you certainly find top-down leadership in the military and in settings like surgeons in the operating room. Although you can't make generalizations in industrial settings, I have found that generally in a top-down organization, the leader's approach often seems appropriate to the comparatively narrow skill level of the overall workforce.

The top-down organization is usually headed by a strong leader. Being a strong leader is good. But even the strongest leader in a top-down organization cannot shut out the rest of the world. The most successful leaders in today's top-down organizations are those who continually get knowledge from the outside, add new people to their organization periodically who did not come up through the ranks, and have open discussions among executives in which no one is afraid to give an opinion even though the CEO will probably make the final decision. Wise top-down leaders do "tier skipping" and get to interact with those in the workforce other than those who work directly for them. Town forums and public meetings are often a good way to interact with the workforce without directly circumventing the line organization.

In the top-down organization, it is most critical that the CEO empower the leadership throughout the organization so that operational managers are able to own their piece of the organization, to make decisions, to not be second-guessed all the time, to be willing to take measured risks, and to not be afraid to fail. The top leader needs to create an organization that fosters these attributes.

Top-Down Leadership: The Military Context

Military leadership, as I have stated previously, usually operates in top-down fashion, and so does leadership in large industrial corporations that employ former military officers as executives. For example, when Jack Welch was CEO of GE, he had great success in recruiting military officers and grooming them for corporate leadership. "It is easy to go from the military to the corporate side," he says. "We had fantastic success hiring junior military officers, or JMOs. We had 1,600 in the company when I left GE." Welch made these remarks at the Wharton School, which he visited in May 2005 to speak about his book, *Winning*, which he coauthored with his wife, Suzy.

Robert (Bob) L. Nardelli, a former GE executive who in January 2007 stepped down as the CEO of Home Depot, implemented the same strategy at the Atlanta, Georgia-based home-improvement retail chain. Nardelli discovered the potential of JMOs while he was still at GE and was operating its transportation business. He found that military officers, who had faced the difficult task of leading and motivating soldiers in tough combat situations, had many of the basic leadership skills needed to run GE's transportation operations.

As a result, when Nardelli left GE (following Jeff Immelt's ascension as Welch's successor) to join Home Depot, he replicated the program there. As an article[1] in *Fast Company* magazine notes, the company recruited 340 military officers for its Store Leadership Program in 2004. This was a departure from the past, when most of Home Depot's in-store leaders were experts in hardware. The company, which has 2,000 stores, recruited the JMOs at military outplacement fairs, put them through two years of leadership training aimed at building business and corporate skills, and then gave them the responsibility of running a store that might have $40 million in sales and as many as 150 employees.

Ironically, Nardelli's departure from Home Depot in early 2007 also reveals some of the pitfalls of top-down leadership, about which I will say more later in this chapter. According to observers, Nardelli steadily alienated his supporters on the Home Depot board of directors, including those who had helped recruit him to run the company. Barry Henderson, an equities analyst at T. Rowe Price, the Baltimore, Maryland-based mutual fund company, told the online management journal *Knowledge@Wharton*, "Nardelli made two big mistakes at Home Depot: He alienated employees and angered stockholders." It's important, however, to make a distinction between Nardelli's policies and his particular management style. Generally, his policies began to turn Home Depot around. But even the most determined top-down leaders have to understand the human dynamics of those they lead.

As reported in *Knowledge@Wharton*, "The Home Depot culture is distinct in retail," Henderson said, describing it as having been "extremely entrepreneurial and very customer focused" when Nardelli arrived. Nardelli concentrated on overhauling Home Depot's business processes, which did need to be addressed, but he "overfocused" on the processes and swept aside the elements that made Home Depot special. Nardelli angered people by firing long-time Home Depot executives and bringing in GE alumni. He also increased the number of less knowledgeable part-time workers at Home Depot's stores, which led to diminished customer service, one of the company's strengths. From the very beginning of his tenure, Nardelli, now 58, "damaged morale, and he was seen as a real threat to the Home Depot culture," Henderson said.[2] In August 2007, Nardelli was appointed CEO of Chrysler, giving him another chance to prove his leadership skills.

Despite Nardelli's departure from Home Depot, the use of former military officers in corporations that employ top-down leadership styles does have its merits. According to Welch, when a JMO does well in running a store, the next step is to give him or her a region to manage. "When you send a JMO to Tuscaloosa, Alabama, or somewhere to run a store," Welch says, "they don't tell you, 'I don't think I want to live there' (they've moved around a lot in their career). These people have just been shot at in Iraq, so location is not the major consideration. If you hire MBAs, they will want to be in New York or Boston or San Francisco; they are more picky. It's nice to have these aggressive JMOs who come out of the academy. It translates very well."

Another Welch protégé, Larry Bossidy, successfully applied the principles of top-down leadership to bring about change after he left General Electric in mid-1991, where he had been the chief operating officer of GE Credit, to join AlliedSignal, now renamed Honeywell after the two companies merged in December 1999.

AlliedSignal had an interesting history. After World War I, Germany controlled many of the world's chemical plants, which created shortages in the U.S. for dyes and chemicals. In response, Eugene Meyer, publisher of the *Washington Post*, joined hands with William Nichols, a scientist, to merge five U.S. chemical companies that had been set up during the 1880s, to form the Allied Chemical and Dye Corp. It later expanded into producing ammonia, and then nylons and refrigerants, and during the 1960s and 1970s, the company got into the oil and natural gas industries. Allied and the Signal companies merged their operations in 1985, thus adding considerably to their aerospace, automotive, and engineering products businesses.[3]

Bossidy believes that for a leader to succeed, she or he has to be good at three things. "You have to be good at strategy, you have to be good with people, and you have to be good in operations," he says. When he arrived at AlliedSignal's headquarters in Morristown, New Jersey, he was horrified. As he explains, "Allied Signal had all three processes. They had a strategic plan; they had a people appraisal process; and they had an operating plan or budget—but they were all done about one inch deep. They had not taken them on in the depth that was required."

Bossidy was soon pushing—and pushing hard—for more depth and rigor in each of these three areas. "We did the strategic plan in far more depth than it had been done before," he says. "We appraised people candidly, which took three or four years to do, as opposed to appraisals that I used to call Olympian appraisals, in which people wrote one page that said nothing. And the metrics were fuzzy. We weren't measuring people accurately. We couldn't tell who was performing and who was not. The budgets had no actions associated with them—they were just a series of numbers with no plans behind them. So just by digging deeper and more comprehensively and thoroughly into each of these areas, we changed the culture."

Bossidy's concentrated focus on these three areas paid off for AlliedSignal. His bio on the Honeywell website notes, "During his tenure with AlliedSignal the company achieved consistent growth in earnings and cash flow, highlighted by 31 consecutive quarters of earnings-per-share growth of 13% or more."

It is hardly surprising that many military officers are able to transition well into leadership positions in the corporate world. The leadership training they receive in the armed forces nurtures a strong foundation for being effective leaders in the corporate context, and they were effectively screened and selected for their leadership potential before they became officers.

Gen. Eric Shinseki, who served as the 34th Chief of Staff of the U.S. Army between 1999 and 2003, and was the first Japanese American to serve in the army's top position, has unique insights into the model of leadership in the army, and why it translates well into corporate leadership. He says leaders need six attributes: high ethical values, selflessness, the ability to communicate, determination, passion, and confidence. "All good leaders have these qualities in common," Shinseki says. "Context tempers these attributes. Good leaders are able to use these qualities to build teams and get willing cooperation and get people to do things. They can see a distant horizon and get others to embrace it."

Shinseki explains that context determines the style of leadership that is needed in different situations. For example, at the lower levels of an organization, leadership may be top down and require greater direction, but as you go higher up the organization, the style becomes less directive and more collaborative. And while a collaborative leadership style works well during normal times, in a crisis this style can become a handicap. "You can afford to be expansive and collaborative in normal times, but in a crisis you have to go from collaborative to directive styles," Shinseki says.

Uriel Reichman, founder and President of the Interdisciplinary Center (IDC) in Herzliya, Israel, says that military leadership demands personal courage, and that makes it applicable in other contexts that require top-down leadership. A former dean of the School of Law at Tel Aviv University, Reichman was an officer in the Israeli Army during the Yom Kippur war in October 1973. "A long time has passed since I was an officer in the paratroopers. I can tell you the most important feeling I had when I led people under fire in the field of combat, and that was the fear of fear," he says. "This was my fear: that I would crack down and would not be able to lead my soldiers in a level-headed and cool way with the right decisions into the skirmish and out again with the maximum number of them alive. That drove me and prevented my succumbing to the horrors of the battlefield. Reichman coped with his "fear of fear by capsulation," as he says. "It is as if you are there and you are not there. You go through a process in which you emotionally move yourself out of the situation, and yet you are logically there."

Reichman explains that leadership in this context "is entirely different from leadership when you are not under fire, and when you are in constant fear of death. When you take an enterprise into your hands, you have a vision, you push it. There isn't fear— there is the joy of doing something different and innovative. It's not the kind of duty-bound heavy responsibility to others and the danger of death. There is the joy of moving forward even when the road you take is full of dangers and perils, and you may fall. But there is a belief and all your energies are working overtime, rather than any part of you being capsulated. You are very creative and responding to the problems you are facing. It is an entirely different feeling and experience showing leadership in combat and showing leadership in competitive noncombatant situations."

According to Reichman, leadership in the military is top down since "there is a hierarchy, and you are not entirely free to move as you want. Of course, there are always some mavericks in the military who disregard its rules and customs and do whatever they think. They are either thrown out of the military, or they are declared to be the most creative generals. But for most of them, the army fits them. It looks for some independence and creativity, but not too much."

Gen. P.X. Kelley had the following lessons to offer about leadership to cadets at the Marine Corps Base in Quantico, Virginia: "Remember, leadership is a personal style. Listen carefully to the principles of leadership we will teach you here at Quantico, but always apply them within the framework of your own personality. Don't try to emulate others. What could be highly successful for one individual could spell disaster for another. Be your own man."

"A successful leader never languishes in the comfort of a swivel chair," he says. "The most important of all troop-leading steps, yet the one most often neglected, is the last—to supervise. And you supervise by being out with and devoting the bulk of your time to our most important product—people. You can always catch up on what you thought was essential paperwork during the evenings or on weekends, but once neglected, you will find it extremely difficult, if not impossible, to catch up on people.

"Don't be a martinet who hides behind his rank and authority to lead. True leaders are respected, never feared. True leaders are compassionate, never abusive. True leaders express their views articulately and, when required, forcefully, but never in demeaning, abusive, or four-letter language. A marine officer who abuses his authority is an absolute coward, for he resorts to fear when he is unable to earn respect."

Top-Down Leadership and Change at Fuji Xerox

Yotaro ("Tony") Kobayashi, chairman of the board of Fuji Xerox, narrates an interesting example of how powerful top-down leadership can be when it is used correctly. Kobayashi, who is based in Tokyo, says Fuji Xerox was formed in 1962 as a joint venture between Fuji Photo Film and Xerox. "As a joint venture, we had licenses from Xerox and a reputation as the local partner of Fuji Photo Film, but otherwise we were starting from scratch," he says. "We were helped by the winds of the times—which at that time were blowing strongly towards the corporate need for modernization, including bringing in top-notch technologies and the best possible office equipment. The Fuji Xerox group had unique products, which were right for the times."

Then the winds changed. In the mid-1970s, Xerox faced a consent decree from the U.S. government and the company was forced to make its technologies available to other companies, leading to a dramatic increase in competition. "After that, the whole environment changed for Fuji Xerox," says Kobayashi. The new competitive market exposed weaknesses at Fuji Xerox that had not been apparent earlier. "There were a couple of major ones. One concerned the company's ability to assess the market objectively. The second involved looking at the data (or numbers) in an objective way. We had to find ways of solving those problems."

To tackle these problems, according to Kobayashi, Fuji Xerox decided to implement a management technique, total quality control (TQC), which others refer to as total quality management (TQM). "This was almost symbolic in putting a lot of emphasis on the data, and setting rational priorities in decision making," Kobayashi says. "We saw conceptually that what TQC was trying to achieve was similar to very basic problem solving, the sort of approach taught at the Wharton School during the 1950s. First, we had to define the problems and then examine the alternatives that could help solve the problems. This was the solution we were ready to implement to get the whole organization behind TQC. That was the management solution."

Then the question of leadership came up. Kobayashi, who was second in command at the company at that time, saw that although rationally the organization was sold on the concepts of

TQC and TQM, "people just did not move much, especially people in middle management and those who were in the corporate offices. This was mainly because, for one reason or another, Fuji Xerox had a very strong corporate culture. And though there were rational and objective aspects of TQC, they could be interpreted in many different ways. I was feeling increasingly desperate, even scared, because if we did not do anything as a company at that time, Fuji Xerox would be doomed to go down to the bottom."

Kobayashi took it upon himself to convince the management that the TQM initiative was not simply one more step for the rational improvement of management processes. Simultaneously with the launch of the quality initiatives, he embarked on an almost evangelical mission to explain to employees at every level that these steps were of do-or-die significance for the company's survival. If the company failed to use the quality initiatives to regain some of the competitive advantages that it had enjoyed before Xerox faced the U.S. government's decree and the market's circumstances changed, it could bring Fuji Xerox down.

Danger can be a strong motivator. By creating a sense of crisis and fear—based on real changes that had occurred in the competitive landscape—Kobayashi's communications helped bring the employees in alignment with corporate goals. As a result, Fuji Xerox not only weathered the storm, but emerged as a stronger organization. Danger often has to be present to cause real, rapid change. It creates an environment where change is possible and essential. When danger is present but certain constituent groups refuse to recognize it soon enough, however, problems arise. The Big 3 auto companies and airlines are two good examples of this.

Let me add a word of caution. While the approach of creating fear around a specific issue can work in the short run in response to a real problem (as it did in the case of Fuji Xerox), I do not favor men or women who lead their troops by trying to instill fear as a "leadership tool." When I was the managing partner of Touche Ross, there was an individual who headed one area who used this approach regularly with his subordinates. He told them that the firm was really against this division and didn't care for their particular group. He implied that they were viewed as second-class citizens. He then positioned himself as their leader by claiming he would represent them and keep bad things from happening to them.

This is a form of negative leadership. It is often used by politicians who claim that their country is about to be attacked by some enemy or that other dire circumstances are about to befall them, and they marshal followers by exploiting those fears. At Touche Ross, this tactic won this person some followers, but it was debilitating to the overall organization. He used the same "scare" approach in dealing with the firm's leadership; if he did not get his way or something he wanted, he would threaten to resign. He did this at least once a year. After a few years of this, when the firm had a real alternative leader ready to go, this person came to me and threatened to resign. I said, "I understand your feelings, and I accept your resignation." He was so shocked he could hardly speak. After his departure, this area of the firm excelled. It finally had a leader who could inspire his team by being enthusiastic about success rather than instilling fear of failure and being discriminated against.

The Pitfalls of Top-Down Leadership

Though top-down leadership may seem simple and straightforward, there is more exposure to problems in this type of leadership than in more collegial types. Probably the greatest potential pitfall is that over a period of time, in the more autocratic form of top-down leadership, CEOs tend to let their egos get in the way because everyone around them is telling them what a great job they are doing. They have a lot of people saying "yes" as opposed to arguing with them, and they never really hear the other side of the story. Then, since they feel they know all the answers, not only to the basic business that they are in, they begin to think they also know the answers to most everything, including global warming, how to deal with North Korea, the diplomatic situations in various parts of the world, and just about any other subject. They begin talking a lot more than they listen. A late stage of this progression is that even when they do get input from others, they say, "Oh we tried that three years ago and it didn't work."

I saw an example of this when I was the dean of The Wharton School of Business at the University of Pennsylvania. We were promoting our Advanced Management program to major local businesses. I contacted the Mellon Bank and talked to a top executive, who told me he would discuss it with some of his people and get back to me. I knew that their leadership style was top-down and insular but hoped that our Wharton program would be sufficiently interesting for them to send some executives for a trial course. But, when he called back, he said they really don't send their people to outside courses. He said they wanted to train them internally in the "Mellon way." This surprised me because a lot of companies were sending their executives to the AMP program so that they could interact with a broad variety of participants and also get new ideas from the outside. The Bank of New York acquired Mellon Financial in December 2006 for $16.5 billion, about $6 billion less than it had offered for the same institution back in 1998.

Another example from my own experience occurred when I headed the Philadelphia office of Touche Ross. Philadelphia was a banking center in the United States probably second only to New York. Touche Ross had a very small office there compared to the other then-Big Eight firms, and we were always looking for business. One of my partners and I met with the CEO of the Girard Bank that was also run in a classic top-down style. We told him we had an idea that would potentially save the bank tens of millions of dollars in taxes. We offered to do a survey and, if we thought our idea would work, proceed to complete the job and get a tax ruling on it. The bank would have to pay us only according to the hours that we spent. If, however, we did the survey and thought it wouldn't work, it would cost the bank nothing. We did not tell the

CEO what our idea was, and he said he would talk to his tax people and get back to us. When he called back, he told us that, even though his tax people didn't know what our idea was, they told him they weren't interested because they would already have looked at any idea that would have saved that much in tax money and either enacted it or rejected it. Girard Bank is now gone.

A final example from my experience may shed some light on the continuing problems in the American auto industry. I lived in Detroit for a number of years and worked on the audits of two of the auto companies. In general, I found that they had very top-down organizations where the top leaders felt they had most of the answers. At that time, in the late '50s and early '60s, the Big Three had the lion's share of the market for automobiles in the United States. Today the situation has changed dramatically: In January 2007, GM, Ford, and Chrysler accounted for a little more than 50% of U.S. auto sales, while the Asian companies—both Japanese and Korean—accounted for more than 40%. Many experts expect this trend to continue. Among the Big Three, Chrysler was bought out by a German auto company, Daimler Benz, in 1998. But thanks to poor sales of Chrysler's minivans and jeeps, Daimler sold Chrysler in 2007 to Cerberus Capital Management, who immediately hired Robert Nardelli, deposed CEO of Home Depot, as CEO of Chrysler. Ford and General Motors have been struggling with high costs, declining sales, and huge losses with even some mention of one or both possibly going into bankruptcy. For the first time it its history, in 2006 Ford hired a CEO from outside the automobile industry with the clear expectation that he will bring fresh ideas to an ingrown company. Cerberus hopes for the same from Nardelli at Chrysler. Toyota has already surpassed Ford as the #2 automobile company in the United States, and despite Detroit's best efforts, many believe that it soon will overtake General Motors to become the largest automobile company in the world. Toyota has talked to Ford about "joint endeavors."

The Ford example points to a related pitfall. Top-down organizations very often form inbred cultures and very strong executive offices. The people in the executive offices are often paid higher than the operational managers who are responsible for the day-to-day operations out in the divisions. This heavily centralized organization can inhibit innovation and an ability to move quickly. It can also limit what information and ideas can pass through a very small filter into the executive office and ultimately to the CEO. The bureaucracy ultimately will stifle the entire organization.

Larry Bossidy, former CEO of Honeywell International, describes another potential pitfall that top-down leaders should be aware of. This is a failure to make sure that the organization executes their strategy. In his words, "There are CEOs who think it is their job to plot strategy. To visit customers. And to have various kinds of community relationships. These are things that are important, but they are not connected with making sure that things that are supposed to happen, happen. There are lots of CEOs who don't like execution. They don't follow up. They expect others to do these day-to-day chores. When the CEO isn't interested in execution, invariably the organization isn't either. And so, in my mind, one of the important qualities of the leader is not just the ability to visualize and articulate that direction, but also to make sure that it happens."

Finally, top-down leaders are prone to the sin of not knowing when it's time to go. In this type of organization, many of the CEOs who have attained the exalted status of having all the answers tend to hang on long after the time when they are still effective. They often also have boards that are rubber stamps for their actions that compound the problem. Knowing when it's time to go can spare a previously successful leader from the ignominy of being fired by a board that has lost patience with declining performance.

Leading in Other Contexts

It is not unusual for top-down leaders to find themselves in other leadership contexts as a part of their regular responsibilities. They are often asked to head organizations other than their primary business—for example, the United Way, Museum Boards of Trustees, and the Business Round Table. In such contexts, any leader who tries to maintain an autocratic style of treating his or her constituents as minions who can be ordered to perform on command is very likely to fail. This is probably the greatest trap into which top-down leaders can fall when they least expect to.

Summary

- Top-down leadership exists mainly in the military and in large industrial corporations that have a strongly hierarchical culture—as also in situations in which a surgeon is leading a team during an operation. If you are a leader in this context, you will find that authority is concentrated in the hands of the leader, who takes command directly and expects orders to be followed without much debate or discussion.

- Even if you are in a top-down organization, in order to be effective, you will find that your leadership style must include some empowerment of subordinates lower down the organizational chain. Unless you do this, the organization will become too top-heavy, and its ability to respond to external change will be limited to your capacity to react to situations.

- Several examples exist to illustrate that top-down leadership can be effective in some circumstances. For example, companies like GE and Home Depot have had a good experience with employing former military officers and empowering them to run a variety of operations. Fuji Xerox employed a top-down initiative to drive through a change aimed at improving quality throughout the organization.

- The major risk of top-down leadership is that as the leader you can get isolated from your constituents and alienate them without realizing it. Beware of becoming a leader who starts believing that you have ultimate knowledge about everything and stops listening and starts believing your own "press." That is often the beginning of the end of sound leadership.

Endnotes

[1] "Home Depot's Hardware Warriors," *Fast Company*, September 2004.

[2] "Home Unimprovement: Was Nardelli's Tenure at Home Depot a Blueprint for Failure?" *Knowledge@Wharton*, January 10, 2007.

[3] Honeywell website (www.honeywell.com/sites/honeywell/ourhistory.htm).

Chapter 4

THE ORGANIZATION OF PEERS: LEADING YOUR EQUALS

The context described in this chapter is in sharp contrast to the top-down leadership described in the preceding chapter. It requires a quite different leadership style, and it is a context with which I have had considerable personal experience, as you will see.

First I describe the management style that is appropriate to this context using my experience leading one of the Big Eight accounting firms (before they became the Big Four). Next I point out potential pitfalls that leaders in this context might encounter. Then I describe other contexts that you might find yourself in when leading an organization of peers that differ and how this can affect your leadership style in those contexts.

Context: The Organization of Peers

One of the most challenging organizations to lead is one in which many people in the organization are nominally equal to the top leader. These include partnerships in law, accounting, management consulting, finance, medicine, and other groups of professionals that include knowledge workers who expect to play a major role in setting the direction of the organization. Often these professionals are in demand and can move to other organizations relatively easily if they become unhappy with their present firm. This puts a high premium on the diplomatic skills of the top leader.

Since the leaders in these organizations are usually chosen by their peers, it is assumed that they have been recognized as right for the job. Once in office, these leaders no doubt have some idea of what needs to be done for the organization to move forward and remain competitive in an often-changing business environment. I believe that the most important means of bringing a group of peers onboard and having them involved in the process of change is to focus on communication—both to and from the peers. This means that you begin by listening to your people, and with their constant input you define a strategic plan or direction that they accept. You assess your people and work with those partners who can help to execute the plan, and you find a way of changing those who can't. Then you pick a team from among the partners who are onboard to execute the plan. It does not stop there. You continue to communicate and measure progress against the plan. Through it all you establish and maintain a position of integrity. Your peers see that you say what you mean and mean what you say. Several years ago I read an interview with Ron Daniels, who led McKinsey, the global consulting firm, from 1976 to 1988. He was asked how he had managed to lead such a large partnership. He replied that it was possible because his colleagues trusted in his integrity. He was absolutely right. If you do this well, the partners most often buy into the plan and its successful execution.

This is neatly summed up by John McKernan, Chairman of Education Management Corporation and former governor of Maine. He says, "Leading one's peers is the greatest challenge and greatest reward for a leader. When you lead your peers, you are leading people who are following you because of a real belief in what you are doing. That means you have expressed a compelling vision in a way that people support, and you clearly have built a trusting relationship because of the fact that your peers agree to follow you. That is why it is one of the most rewarding things when you can bring a cross-functional team to work together on a common vision and to accomplish a common goal."

My own experience at Touche Ross gave me a personal perspective on leading peers, and I will describe this in some detail. The reason I narrate my experience is to give readers a sense of the specific leadership principles and how they can be used in this organizational context with partners and peers.

When I joined Touche Ross in 1956, I knew it was among the world's top accounting and professional services firms. Formed in 1946 as Touche, Niven & Co., it was part of the so-called Big Eight CPA professional services firms. I became a partner in the firm in 1966 and I led the Philadelphia office from 1967 to 1972. That year, I became the managing partner, the title of the chief executive officer of the U.S. firm, and in 1974 I also became the chief executive officer of the international firm. I was 37 and the youngest managing partner in the firm's history and the youngest to ever head one of the large accounting and consulting firms. Don't let that impress you too much because when I assumed that role, I didn't have the foggiest idea how to manage the huge firm. I was counting on Robert Beyer, the outgoing managing partner, who also was my mentor, to give me some on-the-job training.

I found that after a short period, what I had taken on as my first big leadership job was probably one of the most complex organizations anyone could tackle. In fact, Peter Drucker, the well-known management guru, had spent a considerable amount of time with the former managing partner. He wrote that there are some organizations that are so complex that they may be unmanageable. The first to come to his mind were the multinational accounting and consulting firms.

When I became managing partner, the firm had more than 300 offices in 50 countries. At the end of my term 10 years later, we were in 90 countries with more than 400 offices. The organization in each of the countries was financially independent and had its own board. No profit sharing or financial ties existed between the various countries. One of the problems with those 300-plus offices was that they all expected me as the CEO of the U.S. firm and the CEO of the international firm to show up occasionally. How could I do that when showing up just once each year at more than 300 offices would leave little time for anything else? I also had to deal with myriad personalities with different business practices, customs, and mentalities.

In the U.S., a board of directors governed the U.S. firm. The chairman of the board was separate from the CEO and managing partner. There was an executive committee that functioned as the management committee of about 15 people who represented all the various regions and functions of the firm. There was an international executive board made up of the key countries, and an international governing body that included all the countries. I was supposed to "run" the worldwide firm in this context.

Now for the *pièce de résistance*: I had to be elected every year by secret ballot by the partners of the U.S. firm and in my international capacity by the board of the international firm. How many CEOs would like to submit to that? These were my peers and partners whom I was now to lead.

At age 37, with no idea how to manage such a complex organization, I had been elected as the managing partner to take office in about six months. The on-the-job training that I had counted on from Robert Beyer, the previous managing partner, didn't materialize. About four months before I was supposed to take over, he had a stroke and was totally incapacitated.

The firm was somewhat rudderless for a period of weeks, with lots of people calling me up to find out what they should do about some issue or the other. There was even the question of whether my election was now valid because there was a different process for naming an interim managing partner in case the managing partner was incapacitated. After a few weeks of seeing the firm in this condition, I made the unilateral decision to move to the New York office and into an empty office next to Beyer's. I immediately called meetings and sent out memos that in effect said, "I'm here and until Bob Beyer is able to do so, I am acting as managing partner." I wasn't sure of the legal status of what I said. No one had told me to say it and luckily no one questioned it.

And so we started. It wasn't too long after I became managing partner that the firm faced a crisis that threatened its very existence. A liability case we had pending for some time with a West Coast client, Equity Funding, was decided by a jury that assessed damages of $90 million against our firm. There was only one problem. The net worth of our firm was about $50 million and we had $50 million of insurance. If we had to pay this claim, we would have been nearly bankrupt. We later found a way to settle the case for less than $50 million. The SEC was also involved in this case. One fine day, soon after I moved into a new home in a respectable neighborhood in Greenwich, Connecticut, the front page of *The New York Times* business section ran a picture of the chief accountant of the SEC and me with a headline that said, "Touche Ross Censured by SEC." I am sure my new neighbors must have thought I was some sort of a white-collar crook.

This was the leadership challenge I faced as the head of a global professional services firm. Remember that not only did I have to be elected by secret ballot every year by the people I was supposed to lead in an organization that was big and complex, but all the partners really wanted the organization to act like a partnership of equals. To complicate matters even more, the firm operated in an international arena that did not have financial ties between the various firms, and I was not able to determine the compensation of the partners outside the United States. Clearly my first leadership task was to proceed very carefully.

I pointed out at the beginning that the key to leading peers is communication and establishing the personal integrity of the leader. You have to communicate constantly so that people know what is going on. If you don't, rumor mills will take over and you'll be on the defensive all the time. There were p-grams, tri-grams, and all kinds of grams that went to the partners very frequently. These newsletters covered what was going on in the firm, our problems, and new ideas. The idea was for everyone to believe they knew everything that was going on. Obviously, there were many things they didn't know about, but they knew about the most significant issues.

This communication helped to build trust, the foundation of integrity. If the partners believe they can't trust you, you're out even before you start. You have to manage in a very collegial fashion and get as much done as you can while making the decisions that need to be made quickly and making certain things happen. You have to be persuasive, and beyond that, be a good salesperson. You have to find out the goals of the various constituents among the partnerships and help them achieve those goals. You have to show them you can deliver on compensation, and at the same time grow the firm and be competitive against seven other very difficult competitors.

Because it was an international firm, I had to find out what I could do for the Touche Ross partners around the world. In collaboration with them, we set up a system of business referrals from other countries that would enhance the growth and profits of the various firms. We introduced new products to the various firms after frequent consultation. We collaborated on such things as training and other programs with which they needed help.

All of this meant that I had to travel constantly to see people face to face. During my 10 years as CEO, I traveled more than 200,000 miles a year. It may not seem like much until you realize you have to go around the world every month to rack up such miles. I used to go to dinner parties in Greenwich on the weekends. Everybody would ask me where I'd been this week, and I would tell them. They thought all that travel was great, except all I ever saw was a hotel, an office, a restaurant for lunch and dinner, and I was off again to the airport. Any traveling businessperson knows what I am talking about.

Not incidentally, I also had four young children and a wife, and I had to carefully program the time I was going to see them. For instance, I took six weeks' vacation a year—not consecutively—all with the family. No golf. I tried to be home every weekend so that I could be with my family. All the rest of the time I was working. I had an apartment in New York and I had to go to two rubber-chicken dinners on average a week when I was not traveling as it was generally one of our clients who was being honored. If you add it up over the 10 years, it adds up to 1,000 rubber-chicken dinners.

In the early months after becoming managing partner, I formulated a vision for Touche Ross that we had to "be the best" among the global professional services firms—and we had to be "one firm." If we were one firm, we had to think as one team—and each time we wanted to land a major account, we had to pull out all the stops and work together. Working with a group of partners, we came up with a plan that would help us become the preeminent firm among our peers. My former colleague John Keydel, who was head of strategic planning at Touche Ross, says, "Russ Palmer came up with the slogan 'Be the Best.' These are energizing words. We developed the p-grams, which were periodical newsletters that communicated a common vision of the firm."

To realize the vision, the firm had to have the right people in the right jobs. This proved to be difficult and painful for a number of partners. Touche Ross originally had been formed in the U.S., and through a series of more than 50 mergers it had become an organization that almost seemed to be a collection of fiefdoms. The partners who had merged their firms into Touche Ross were used to running their own show. Some of them could only be described, to be candid, as prima donnas with mighty egos, and cronyism was rife. If we continued to function as a collection of firms united only by a common name, we would never have been effective in competing successfully against the other Big Eight firms. We had to develop a leadership strategy that could help us overcome this limitation.

Prima donnas sometimes care only about themselves and not the goals of the organization as a whole. An important part of leadership is that you have to have the strength to redirect them. If you don't, they will undermine the efforts of countless other sincere and hard-working people. On the other hand, when redirected they can be a significant positive force. They didn't get to be prima donnas by being untalented.

47

I encountered such situations from time to time after 1974 (when I became the managing director and CEO of Touche Ross International). We had a crisis in the office in France. The firm there was run by an individual who ran everything and couldn't be redirected—he had no real partners. He was not interested in growth. Eventually we had to ask him to retire and we would buy out his interest. This was difficult to accomplish since we didn't own the French firm and didn't have line authority over this individual, and the other firms, particularly in Europe, were watching the situation very closely. The leverage we had over the firm came from the fact that we accounted for about 50% of their business in referral work from other countries. If we pulled the business, they would have been in deep trouble. In the end, the firm had no choice but to retire the man if it wanted to remain viable.

Another problem was that some partners had become alcoholics. Others had different problems that interfered with their work. We had to tell them that they should stop, or they would be asked to leave. It had a huge impact because people were watching. When you do something like this, word spreads around the whole firm. It has a wildfire effect. You had better be right in what you do or it will have a detrimental backlash.

Once we had established a common vision for the firm, and also come up with a common set of goals, we had to figure out how to motivate people to achieve them. In a partnership, this can be quite complicated—but we did it through managing the compensation process, along with other methods. In both the international firm and the U.S. firm, we had a strategic plan. I kept the boards informed about the plan, and the execution was done through the executive committee. In the U.S. the compensation system of the partners was tied directly to the strategic plan. We had six major areas on which the compensation system was based: profit, growth, quality, people, interaction with the outside world, and what they did for the firm as opposed to their specific job or office. We constantly measured the execution of the strategic plan and the related specific plans for the various areas.

We adjusted our compensation system from time to time as we changed short-term goals depending on what we were emphasizing during that year. However, our long-term plan remained the same: to drive our firm from being the smallest, newest member of the Big Eight—and one that some people did not even consider a member of the Big Eight—to one that was at least in the middle of the pack. We had to outperform all our competitors to get there.

One year, for instance, we said we would focus on strengthening our partnership. We had more than 50 mergers, and there were clearly some partners who were not up to the standards of the partnership we were building and who were not equipped to perform at the level that was required. It is commonplace today for partners in the Big Four firms to be "retired" early, but in the 1970s it was a rare occurrence, particularly 150 of them over a short period of time. But we did it, and we were a stronger partnership as a result of that move.

We accomplished this task by asking everybody on the executive committee to bring a list of the partners they felt should be "outplaced." We put the lists together, talked about those who were on the composite list, and brought the final list down to the people who would be asked to retire. Generally I agreed with the names on the final list, with one exception that I will describe in the next section on pitfalls. The rest were eased out of the firm.

A source of our strength was diversity among the partners. Probably 30% or 35%—one-third of our partners—were of the Jewish faith, by far the largest number of the Big Eight firms. We also had a very large group of the Catholic faith, and we had all sorts of minorities represented. They had one thing in common: They were good at what they did.

We had people with beards, people with mustaches, people of different nationalities and ethnic backgrounds. There were lots of women in high positions and considerable representation of minorities. And remember, this was in the 1970s. Several of the firms made a big thing of the fact during that time that they had starting hiring women. We had had women in our firm since it was founded in 1946. In fact, on my first job I worked for a woman. We had a great number of women partners when certain other firms weren't even hiring women. Now more than 50% of the new hires in many accounting firms are women.

Our partners were good not only because they were diverse but also because they were extraordinary people. I have often said that extraordinary people aren't ordinary in more ways than one. In other words, you know that someone like Pablo Casals is one of the greatest cellists in the world, but in every other way you expect him to be just like your next-door neighbor. Well, that's not true. Extraordinary people not only are extraordinary in what they do best but are generally quite different from your ordinary everyday citizen, and as the leader you have to understand and to a great degree accommodate that. Keeping our best people also meant that we had a policy of up or out. That was it. Either you became a partner or you were moved out of the firm along the way. And to get to be a partner, you did it based on merit, intelligence, and what you could contribute to the firm. We didn't have any nepotism. In fact, we didn't even allow relatives in the firm. But I recall we did make an exception for two excellent brothers, one in the San Francisco office and one in Denver.

We believed that even if we had the best people, we needed to keep them on the leading edge with a continuing professional development program. This wasn't always easy. In fact, it was very difficult to lead our professionals in a new direction, just as it is in other kinds of organizations. In the late 1970s, computers had just begun to come into vogue in our profession and were starting to be used for auditing. We bought a lot of computers and gave them to our young people and had classes for everyone so that they could use this new tool that made auditing more efficient and less expensive. Later we did a survey on how many people were using computers in auditing, and we found out it was still a very low percentage. When we looked into this situation and tried to find the reason, we found that it was because the partners didn't want audits to be done this way; they didn't understand computer auditing. Young people wanted to use computers, but the senior partners asked them to perform audits the same old way.

At the annual meeting of all partners in charge of the 80 domestic offices, when they walked into the meeting room the first morning, there was an Apple computer at every desk. They sat down. We talked about demonstrating how useful the computers were, and then we had someone come in and show them how to use the computers. After the annual meeting, we shipped every computer to either the home or the office of the partner in charge, depending on their preference. I asked them to write me every month and tell me what they had done with their computer. At the end of six months, if they had not used the computer, they had to send it back to me.

At first, they all wrote to me and everyone said they were using their computers. In fact, I think they all did, but only to a modest degree. But after they had used their computers for a while, in their minds they became experts. No one wrote me and said they weren't using their computer. Then they began to tell all their other partners that computers were great and should be used in auditing. That was how we broke through the logjam on computers, which are now used as an integral part of every audit. As a matter of fact, when you see a staff person from one of the Big Four firms today, they all have computers—often laptops—that they carry around with them or pull on little trolleys. Today computers have become as essential to auditing as adding machines or calculators were in the old days.

We were the antithesis of the Price Waterhouses and Arthur Andersens of those days. Andersen certainly had a fine firm, but they had the same doors on every one of their offices, no matter where you went in the world. And when you went in, all the people you met looked the same. I recall that Arthur Andersen would tell their clients that you could go anywhere in the world and meet U.S. partners in all their offices who knew about U.S. customs and doing business in the U.S.

We stressed the international strengths of the firm to clients and told them that we had a German firm in Germany and an

Arab firm in the Arab League countries and a Japanese firm in Japan. These were indigenous firms that understood the business practices of those countries. And yes, we did have a couple of Yanks seconded to those firms who provided a friendly point of contact with headquarters in New York for the indigenous partners. And those partners at the same time allowed the clients to gain a broad perspective on the international market.

As a result of this international strategy, in many years the biggest single growth in the U.S. firm was from major foreign companies that had referral work to be done in the United States. As business globalized even more in the 1980s and 1990s, an increasing amount came from foreign companies that were audited by our associated firms in Germany, Japan, the UK, and so forth.

When the Arab League in the 1970s announced a boycott of any firm that made contributions to or did business with Israel, they particularly targeted the Big Eight. All the firms were very concerned about this because if you couldn't do business in the Arab League countries, you couldn't serve many of your multinational clients such as the big oil companies. We talked about this and decided that no one should tell us how to run our firm. In fact, we decided to make a $1 million pledge publicly to the United Jewish Appeal in New York. We never were put on the boycott list.

The cultural differences between Touche Ross and the other global accounting firms were so pronounced that even external observers picked up on them. As author Mark Stevens wrote in his book *The Big Eight*, "As a group Touche Ross partners are different than those at Peat Marwick, Coopers, Arthur Young, and the like. Touche Ross people tend to be more casual, relaxed, and candid. There is a greater diversity here. One does not get the feeling that a stamping machine turns out the Touche Ross partners according to a master plan. At a single meeting at Touche Ross national office one finds a brash cigar chomping New Yorker, a gesturing Japanese, a reserved Texan, and a jovial toothy midwestern. There's a Jew, a Jap, a Catholic, and a Wasp."

As my former colleague Carl Griffin, who was the chairman of the board of the firm when I was managing partner, recalls, "We attracted young, energetic people who were interested in taking on the giants and willing to do things with fewer resources. We were not as big and were not making as much money as the other Big Eight firms were, but we had a great desire to show the other firms how great our firm was. We had a strong sense of competition with the outside world—of how good we were while fighting with fewer chips. We wanted to prove we had new ways of doing things."

Being small and ambitious, we had to be innovative. Back in those early days in the 1970s, there wasn't much advertising done by the professional services firms. In fact, there was a prohibition against it. One day Apple called me and asked me if I would appear in an ad for them. This ad ran for about six months in every major business magazine, on TV, and such. There was quite a bit of consternation among some in the profession who saw it as advertising. I said it was Apple that was advertising. I hadn't paid anybody nor did anybody pay us to be a part of it. All the senior leaders of the other firms grumbled, while the younger people in their firms wondered why their managing partners weren't featured in ads. We continued to lead the way in innovation, and today, for instance, all the accounting firms advertise regularly.

In the end, after 10 years, we had more than 400 offices in 90 countries. That year, in 1982, the largest company that changed auditors was NBC, and we got it in competition with all other members of the Big Eight. We also had arguably the best strategic consulting group in the Big Eight. Don Curtis, who led consulting and who was a great strategist, said somewhere during the mid-to-late 1970s we became viable as a firm and a legitimate member of the Big Eight.

In his book *The Big Eight*, Mark Stevens, whom I quoted previously, observed, "Touche Ross is the one firm its newly aggressive competitors love to hate. That's because Touche Ross is an imaginative and energetic CPA firm with its sights set squarely on today and its mind focused more on tomorrow than yesterday. It is a street-smart gutsy firm with few formalities, a top-notch staff, intelligent and innovative partners and hot prospects for continued growth...Touche Ross with its feet on the ground [is] prowling the city for business."

We definitely built a partnership that is very difficult to duplicate in today's world because the firms are much bigger. They have to be run much more as a corporation than a partnership. After several mergers and acquisitions, Touche Ross is now part of a much larger firm in the Big Four. In October 2003, the combined firm adopted the brand name of Deloitte, though the legal name remains Deloitte & Touche.

The leadership style that served Touche Ross in the 1970s still has key elements such as emphasizing integrity and constant communication that can serve large peer-based organizations today. The problem, however, is that often firms are not run that way due to their size. As a result, people don't feel like true partners and they leave the organization.

Before I turn to describing some of the pitfalls I personally experienced at Touche Ross, I want to add a word about another kind of organization of peers. This is the world of higher education in which every professor considers himself or herself a part of the leadership of the university. And this is nowhere more evident than in a business school. But there are just enough differences between a university and a partnership that I devote Chapter 8, "The Academic Organization: Learning from the Wharton Experience," to a close examination of how a dean of a major business school negotiates the shoals of a group of highly brilliant and highly opinionated business professors. There are lessons in that chapter that I believe can apply to a range of similar kinds of organizations.

Was Touche Ross's climb without problems and mistakes? Of course it wasn't. As we talk about pitfalls, let me start with two examples from my Touche Ross days.

Potential Pitfalls of Leading Peers

One of the deepest pitfalls I think that can befall a leader of partners is to forget the cardinal rule of carefully listening to them and bringing them into the decision-making process on changing the organization. There were two times that immediately came to mind when I was faced with this problem—one of which ended successfully and the other of which definitely didn't.

You will remember that during my tenure as managing partner, I asked the members of the executive committee to make a list of those partners they thought would not be able to contribute to the new strategic direction we had agreed on. When we sat down together to compare the lists, I agreed with all the names but one. The risk I faced was that I might be seen as acting autocratically instead of collegially.

Here's what happened. One person whose name was on the list was a partner named Dennis Mulvihill. He had a Ph.D., and the reason his name was on it was not that he wasn't good—it was that we no longer needed the job he did. I told the executive committee that I was taking Mulvihill off the list. There were some grumbles among the group and a few people asked why. I told them, "I just believe it's the right decision."

After that a rumor went around that Denny Mulvihill had something on me, which was supposedly why I wouldn't let the committee put him on the list. Nothing could have been further from the truth. You see, only I knew that Mulvihill had inoperable terminal cancer and was going to die. He didn't want anyone else to know, so I had to handle it in a very uncollegial fashion. Mulvihill had heard he was on the list, and when I called him in and told him that he wasn't, he wept in my office for five minutes. Then he said, "Thank you," and left. Though the immediate reaction among the partners was that I had acted without taking their views into account, in the end they understood. In fact, I think that my compassion for Denny Mulvihill actually helped to build trust in my approach to leadership.

The other pitfall that I didn't avoid came in my 10th year, 1982. I made a serious mistake in the planning for my successor. It just shows why you don't want to stay around too long because you quit listening. We had a 10-year rule stating that no managing partner who survived the annual voting that long could be in office more than 10 years, and the nominating committee was in the process of determining who would be the next managing partner. I thought it was a good rule and I was ready to do something different. The board had been kind enough to set up my retirement so that after 10 years, at the age of 47, I could retire as though I were 65 years old, which meant I was able to get my retirement payout over about 15-plus years and at the same time go on to something new.

The chairman of the nominating committee came to me after they had deliberated for some time and told me that the board wondered if I would consider an extension over the 10 years. He said they could get the partnership agreement changed to allow that. I thanked him, but said it was time to move on. I had previously proposed to the nominating committee that they nominate two people jointly: one as chairman of the board and one as managing partner. Though we already had this structure, I proposed that the duties of the two positions be reconfigured. The nominee I proposed for chairman of the board was great with clients and the outside world; my nominee for managing partner had a great amount of respect from the partners, and his integrity was of the highest caliber. At that time Goldman Sachs had John Whitehead and John Weinberg as co-managing partners, and I said, "Why can't this work for us too? The chairman needs to stay outside, the managing partner needs to stay inside. It's going to work beautifully."

A great number of partners told me that this dual situation wasn't going to work even though the incumbent chairman of the board and I had had similar roles for 10 years. Many in particular said they didn't think my nominee for chairman of the board was the right person for the job. In fact, a meeting was called during which many of the key leaders of the firm discussed how they could stop him from becoming chairman. I found out about the meeting and went in and gave my thoughts, and then said, "Now I'll leave and let you discuss all this."

My serious mistake was in not listening to the views of the other partners. They were right about my suggested nominees, who were eventually appointed. The chairman of the board didn't stay on the outside but got into internal operations of the firm, and the managing partner didn't stay on the inside but wanted a role in the outside world. So, I'd done a lot of good things at Touche Ross but I bungled the succession. What we should have done was dropped down another tier and taken a younger person who was in his or her late 30s or early 40s just as I had been when I was chosen. Looking back, I regret the decision, but I equally regret that I violated one of my cardinal rules and didn't listen to people whom I respected.

Before I end, I would like to sound a warning against two more pitfalls that leaders must guard against. When they have to lead partners and peers who have relatively narrow specializations, leaders need a broad view. In other words, they must be generalists who know a good deal about many things. One of the problems in today's society is that we develop more and more people with narrowly specialized knowledge. I heard a well-known CEO tell students at the Wharton School that they needed to learn everything about one highly specialized area, and then they could go to Wall Street and make a lot of money. That may be true, but I doubt if that approach would ever enable them to rise to the top leadership of a Wall Street firm. The best subject from an educational standpoint for a leader is the study of history. Reading biographies is also particularly helpful.

Leaders in most situations need to be generalists who have a background in the area they are leading; for example, a doctor in healthcare, or an engineer in manufacturing. The best education, for instance, for a businessperson is a strong liberal arts undergraduate program and then a graduate business program.

The other danger to guard against is hubris. I know that we talked about this in a previous chapter, but it's widespread enough to mention again in the context of leading peers. This is more difficult than it may sound. When you are a leader, you have everyone congratulating you and telling you how smart you are. You are surrounded by people who accept most things—if not everything—you say, even though they may not completely believe them. You see articles about yourself in newspapers and magazines. You are invited to speak at important events. Cameras and microphones are thrust at you when you speak, and your words are widely publicized. After a while, as a leader you start to believe that all they are saying about you is true.

You begin to believe that the reason people hang on your words is that you are a brilliant speaker and that you have incredibly good ideas. The real story is probably that you are being asked to speak at an event because you are a so-called "big name," and your presence may help draw more people to attend. It's also easy to forget that someone else wrote your speech, and that the clever ideas in it and the elegant turns of phrase are often not yours. When this happens, as a leader you may start thinking that you know a lot about everything no matter what the subject is, and that you are almost always right.

Some leaders think that just because they know how to make automobile engines, it makes them world experts about medicine, space exploration, terrorism, Social Security, the avian flu, and just about any other topic they are asked about. Of course, if the person the leader is speaking with knows anything about the subject, that person will soon realize that the leader's knowledge is shallow. Who would want to follow such an egocentric, know-it-all person?

This mindset is fatal. As a leader, you will find that it will work against you no matter what kind of organization you are trying to lead, but it is especially toxic in an environment in which you have to lead partners and peers. When leaders develop such an attitude, they stop listening to others because they believe they know the answers already, so listening is just a time waster. They don't realize that their partners and peers don't respect their arrogance or their pompous attitude.

Leaders who have this mindset find it exceptionally hard adjusting to reality after they move out of leadership positions. For some time afterward, they act as they did when they were in the leader's role, but they don't understand why people don't put up with it anymore. They suddenly find that the people at the old company don't call them, and after a while people don't even recognize them. They may play a lot of golf, but they are not really happy. This might sound like a harsh view, but we all know people like this—who go though life thinking they know all the answers. It's not a way of creating and sustaining followers. It is ultimately extremely detrimental to the leader.

Leading in Other Contexts

Leading a group of partners can be an ideal training ground for other contexts in which these leaders may find themselves. Among these may be association committees, standards commissions, government advisory boards, and university boards of governors. All these contexts will almost certainly bring together other leaders whose egos and expectations will not be unlike those of the leader's own organization. There should be no surprises for leaders in these contexts, and if they have been successful at home, they stand a good chance of being equally successful abroad.

Leading an organization of peers does not mean that the leader can be collegial or ultrademocratic at all times. There will be times when you have to exercise your own judgment and impose your will upon your peers—as I did, for example, in Denny Mulvihill's case—because you may be aware of facts that are not public knowledge. In other circumstances—for example, during the legal crisis that Touche Ross faced soon after I took charge at the firm—the situation may not allow time for much debate and deliberation: Decisions need to be made swiftly. In short, even when you are leading your peers, exceptional situations are bound to come up in which the consultative, consensus-building leadership style won't work and the leader must exercise authority. Knowing when to tighten the reins in your hands and when to relax them requires experience, but fundamentally it calls for judgment—and in the end, that is a very key element in leadership.

Summary

- Leadership of peers or partners demands that you exercise a high degree of diplomacy and collegiality because the partners will expect to play a significant role in setting the direction of the organization.
- As a leader of peers, you will probably have a general idea of what kind of strategic direction is needed for the organization, but you must listen carefully to the opinions of the other partners in setting specific goals before attempting to implement the strategy.
- You will find that open and constant communication among the partners and leader is essential to successfully leading peers.
- Your constant and open communication with your peers will establish your integrity and built trust in your capacity to lead.
- Execution of a new strategic direction requires that you identify those partners who are ready and able to help implement it and to move those who aren't.
- A new strategic direction usually requires innovation and you must foster a spirit of innovation among the partners.
- Your style needs to make your partners feel that you believe they are your peers.
- Watch out for the hubris that may overtake you after you have led your peers successfully and now think that you know everything there is to know.

Chapter 5

THE ORGANIZATION IN CRISIS: TURNING DANGER INTO OPPORTUNITY

No matter what kind of an organizational context you may be leading, it's almost certain that you will have to contend with a major crisis at some time. When it arrives, you must take charge yourself no matter what style you may have employed before. A crisis needs quick and decisive action that only you as the leader can provide.

In this chapter, I describe the context of leading in a crisis using several examples, some of which were handled well and some of which were botched. It may come as a surprise, but I also describe how a crisis can be turned into an opportunity to move the organization forward more quickly than it would have moved without the crisis.

Context: The Organization in Crisis

As a leader, you must recognize that there always will be crises. The only question is how dire they will be. It is part of your job to deal with these situations—you are the person in charge.

During a crisis, leadership becomes very concise. Leaders have little time to deliberate over and discuss decisions. They have to take the reins of the organization directly into their hands and insist, "Do it, and do it now," as leaders in top-down organizations are accustomed to doing. Leaders need to formulate a plan to cope with the crisis. It's ideal if they have developed the plan before the crisis occurs—or at least done some general crisis planning before the fact, if not for this specific crisis. But too often this has not happened and leaders have to react on the run. There is no time for collegiality or even delegation. The situation calls for execution—rapid execution—while being calm under fire. If the team already has great regard for the leader, it makes things easier. But if people are unsure about the leader or have doubts about his or her leadership qualities, that makes execution much more difficult.

Larry Bossidy, the former CEO of Honeywell, captures this reality when he says that during a crisis a leader's style must change: "It becomes much more focused, and much more hands-on.... The leader directly takes command of the ship, and there's not as much delegation as might occur in the running of the business on a normal basis."

Jock McKernan, the former governor of Maine, points out that people's expectations of their leaders also change. "You can make the case that during normal, calmer times, constituents look for a different kind of leader than during a crisis," he says. "During a crisis, you need a leader with a clear sense of direction, tremendous decisiveness, someone who has a plan, and who is a good communicator so that the team knows what is at stake. You need someone who will stand in front of internal and external constituents and communicate constantly so that misinformation does not fill the vacuum."

A good example of this kind of leader is the former New York mayor Rudy Giuliani. During Giuliani's time in office until late 2001, he received lots of positive and negative press. The world got to see his true colors, though, during the September 11, 2001, crisis. In Giuliani's book, titled *Leadership*, he tells the story of his immediate reaction when he heard that the World Trade Center's first tower had been struck. Initially it was unclear what kind of plane had struck the building—and whether it was an accident or an act of terrorism—but Giuliani wanted to check that out in person. He decided to go to the World Trade Center directly because he believed in evaluating each scene of crisis personally—so as not to miss important information. Giuliani was already at the scene when another plane hit the second tower some 15 minutes later—and then he knew it was not an accident.

This kind of hands-on approach is the hallmark of what people expect from their leaders during a crisis. According to McKernan, Giuliani "gave a clear sense of direction, he was able to communicate, he had a plan, he was constantly talking to the press and on television about what was going to happen next. That played to the strength of his personality and his character."

The textbook case of a leader of a large organization dealing effectively with a crisis is, of course, James Burke, the former CEO of Johnson & Johnson, who responded to the well-known Tylenol crisis. Seven people in the Chicago area died in 1982 because a saboteur had laced the drug with cyanide. Burke acted swiftly and decisively. He did not try to manage the crisis long-distance or by telephone. He went directly to the site of the incident to make sure he understood firsthand what the problem was. He gave news conferences and went on television to assure the public that Johnson & Johnson was doing everything possible to remove the potential danger from store shelves. He became the face of J&J to the public. The decision to quickly withdraw the drug from the market was an expensive one for the company to make. But Burke understood what was at stake: the public's confidence in all the J&J products. As a result of Burke's hands-on attention and ability to focus the organization on the situation, J&J emerged from the Tylenol crisis with its reputation intact, and perhaps even enhanced. Those who had predicted the death of the Tylenol brand were proved wrong. Once the crisis had passed, the company regained and increased its sales.

The Tylenol crisis broke suddenly. Other crises ooze rather than break—they build over time and they can present leaders with a do-or-die situation. Xerox, whose name is synonymous with photocopying, is among the best-known brand names in global business. In the 1990s, it undertook a major initiative to bring the company into the fast-changing digital age. After a period of euphoria toward the end of the decade, its situation took a turn for the worse. By 2000, the company was under siege, and questions were being raised about its ability to survive. Revenues—$19.2 billion in 1999—were flat; earnings were plunging; and the company was caught in such a severe cash crunch that its ability to sell commercial paper to pay its bills was impaired. There was talk of the company declaring bankruptcy under Chapter 11. The firing of CEO Richard Thoman, a former IBM executive, in May 2000 and his replacement by Paul Allaire, who had led Xerox through most of the 1990s, had done little to restore the stock market's confidence. The price of Xerox shares, which traded for $64 in May 1999, dropped sharply, and on October 24, 2000, it closed at a little more than $8.

That same month, Anne M. Mulcahy was named president following Thoman's departure. Mulcahy and Allaire quickly announced a turnaround program. It included cutting $1 billion in costs and raising between $2 billion and $4 billion through the sale of assets. Among other steps, Xerox said it would sell its China operations as well as part of its ownership in Fuji Xerox— a joint venture in Japan that serves much of Asia—and other Xerox concerns.[1]

One factor that helped Mulcahy enormously is the credibility she commanded within Xerox. Mulcahy had started her career in Xerox in 1976 as a sales representative and worked her way to the top. She put her experience to work after becoming president and started by listening at length to customers, employees, and other constituents. They told her they felt that Xerox was losing focus, getting involved in projects at random rather than those that were most profitable. At the same time, Mulcahy had to negotiate with nearly 60 banks to renew the company's lines of credits. If those negotiations failed, Xerox would have to declare bankruptcy. She convinced all but two of the bankers—both of whom refused to change their minds. So Mulcahy called upon Sandford Weill, head of Citigroup, whom she regarded as the most influential person in the banking industry, and explained her situation. "While I sat there, he picked up the phone and called both banks," she later said. Mulcahy got her loan.

Dealing with crises often involves drastically cutting costs, and Mulcahy undertook the painful task of reducing the number of employees at Xerox from about 80,000 to 58,000. Among the initiatives that she cut was an inkjet printer division in which Xerox (which invented laser printing technology) thought it no longer had a competitive advantage.

During the worst of times, though, Mulcahy made sure that Xerox did not cut funding for research and development, which were vital for the company to introduce new products and achieve long-term growth. She saw R&D as "the light at the end of the tunnel"—and she was right. As the company's perform-ance improved, these R&D projects helped generate new products that could contribute to the top line and the bottom line. By 2005, three-quarters of revenues came from products intro-duced during the previous two years. Under her leadership, Xerox went from a loss of $273 million in 2000 to a profit of $859 million on sales of $15.5 billion in 2004. The company's stock price rose by 75% over a period of five years.[2] Xerox has continued to perform well under Anne Mulcahy's leadership. According to the company's 2006 annual report, net income increased further to $1.2 billion on revenues of $15.8 billion in 2006.

During a visit to Wharton in November 2005, Mulcahy gave a lecture in which she described her experience at Xerox and how she and her team turned the company around.

When asked about her approach to leadership, Mulcahy said: "It's most important to play to your strengths and not to conform to someone else's image of leadership. It allows you to have integrity of style and consistency of character. I don't think I'm a different leader today than I was when I had my first manage-ment job. I'm very direct. I'm less into management than I am into working with teams and solving problems. So I'm very engaged and involved, but also, I think, I encourage others to have a lot of fun. Even during our darkest days, I'm big on, 'It's a job, so lighten up and don't confuse life and work.' I put a lot of energy into my work, but it's still work."

Following her lecture, Mulcahy said what made the cost-cutting initiatives work was that employees around the company participated in them directly and enthusiastically. "There was a real consciousness about incredible things, silly things, but they were symbolic," she said. "There was no longer any free coffee. They cut off all the people who watered plants...anything they could think of. There were literally no free meals. We did not do anything that included a meal at the company for 18 months. No lunches, no breakfasts. But we tried to make it consistent throughout the company, up and down, as well. There weren't 'haves' and 'have-nots.' Everybody was on the same deal."

Anne Mulcahy's leadership during the crisis at Xerox provides an added perspective on my point about the need for a leader in a crisis to take charge. She did take charge but she also understood that to drastically change the organization, she needed to engage key workers in teams that attacked and solved problems. Even a take-charge leader in a crisis must find ways of bringing key players into the process of change.

The Xerox crisis also is an example of another truth about crises in general: It would be a mistake to view every crisis as only something to be overcome. A crisis can also be something that can make you and your organization better. As General George Patton says in the film *Patton* before his first battle with German Field Marshall Erwin Rommel, "All my life I've wanted to lead a lot of men in a desperate battle. Now I'm going to do it." Crises may be troubling times but they are also times of great opportunity. Leadership during a crisis is a solidifying event. It also can be very revealing, especially about people who have not been through a crisis together before. You never know fully about people until you have seen them under fire. During a crisis, leaders really see whom they can count on and whom they cannot. Some so-called loyalists may prove to have been self-serving; other unlikely heroes or heroines may rise to the occasion and come shining through. It is telling how different some people become during a crisis when they see the company's and their own future in danger—as any leader who has been through "the fire" will tell you. No manager understands his team until they have been through a very difficult time together. It is a bonding experience. It's illuminating. It's instructive.

If you accept, as I have said earlier, that a principal task of a leader is to bring about change, you will find that in certain cases a crisis potentially offers a favorable environment to drive change through an organization. The reason, obviously, is that during a crisis the need for change is so palpable. Clearly, something has to change so that the organization—whether it is a company, an educational institution, or a nonprofit—can weather the storm. When directed by a good leader, an organization in crisis can bring about far-reaching changes that survive after it has passed. When a crisis is raging in full-blown fury or even after it has subsided, it offers an opportunity for reshaping an organization. In the direst of situations, it is important for you as a leader not to lose sight of this reality. The Xerox story perfectly demonstrates this.

Another strong woman leader whose job description involved dealing with crises and who views them as opportunities is Marsha (Marty) Evans, former CEO of the American Red Cross. By the very nature of her work, she was constantly coping with crises caused by natural or man-made disasters, but even before she joined the Red Cross, as an admiral she helped the Navy deal with the notorious Tailhook scandal. She headed the Task Force looking into that crisis. As you may remember, that scandal involved charges of sexual harassment in the Navy, and it led to widespread changes regarding the treatment of women in the armed forces.

Evans believes that it is "a leader's responsibility to be constantly preparing an organization for crisis. You can't foresee all the crises; there will be some that will come out of left field. But the time when you don't have a crisis is when you need to be preparing the organization to face it."

How does the leader prepare the organization for crisis before it happens? According to Evans, you do it through constant efforts to evaluate all kinds of risks. "I am a huge believer in risk assessment," she says. "A lot of work is now being done in corporate America where the idea of risk is being extended beyond financial risk models to other kinds of risk, such as reputational and regulatory risk. Those broader definitions are really important. You cannot foresee the future, but you can get ahead of a lot of the issues by a fairly systematic analysis of what could present a risk to the organization."

The Red Cross conducts such risk assessments during the year, and other companies and organizations need to do no less. For example, says Evans, the Red Cross evaluates issues such as whether, if there were to be a major disaster, its IT systems would have the capacity to deal with the influx of public donations. "Asking those kinds of questions and not being satisfied until you have the answer is something that you have to do 365 days a year," she says. "That is critical."

Evans captures the essence of how a crisis can be an opportunity when she says, "There is a blessing in a crisis." She continues, "You sometimes—not always, but sometimes, when it is severe enough—have a situation where people are willing to do whatever needs to be done to get beyond the crisis. Then you can do things that should have been done two or three years ago. No one likes to have an organization that they have been in for 20 years and which they love being pilloried in the media. But to deal with the crisis, you have to have a solid plan.

"I have found that in dealing with crises, I cannot let myself get mired down in the little details. I have to stay scanning the environment. The tsunami is a perfect example. Early on, I was concerned that we were not spending money fast enough, because we were working with the International Red Cross. So I made the decision that we would partner with the World Food Program so that we could begin emergency feeding. Now, this is not a part of the Red Cross's mission, but I made the decision anyway. That kept us out of public jeopardy because we were able to report that we had committed $50 million early on to feeding. It was not a popular decision, but in hindsight it was an important decision that helped keep public support for the Red Cross."

Evans offers some sound advice that sums up the essence of leading during a crisis. "Leading in a crisis means imagining what the worst case might be," she says. "Then you have to build upon your past experience to anticipate what that might entail. After that you get out in front of it and try to avert the crisis, or if it hits, have a good, strong implementation plan in place." Leaders who do this—and follow the cardinal rule that they must communicate constantly with internal and external constituents—will be able to weather the crisis and emerge stronger from it.

Leadership in crisis is an area where leaders must shine. They are clearly in control of the situation. They move decisively, effectively, with sureness of purpose while instilling confidence in their subordinates that they know what they need to do.

A crisis tests a leader's capacity to lead as perhaps no other situation can. Even if the leader's efforts to resolve the crisis fail, that failure offers useful lessons.

Potential Pitfalls of Leading During a Crisis

Probably the biggest pitfall that leaders can fall into is not recognizing that a crisis is brewing before it's too late. Over the years, I have often seen companies that may be heading for the precipice, but they don't know it because they are in denial. Often these are companies that have been around for quite some time, and that may have been successful in the past, but they aren't changing with the times. They think they have all the answers, but they face an erosion in perspective that one day is bound to lead to a severe crisis.

Today, the automobile business offers a prime example of a U.S. industry that seems to have been in denial and has failed to keep up with the times. As far back as the 1970s—but even more so in the 1980s—it was clear that foreign carmakers, especially the Japanese, were capturing young drivers with small, fuel-efficient, and inexpensive cars. These were the car drivers of the future and they weren't buying American cars because our automakers didn't believe they could make money on small, inexpensive vehicles. Did anybody at that time believe that Toyota would probably be, in the not-too-distant future, the biggest auto company in the U.S.— and therefore in the world? Could anybody believe the percentage of the American car market that is now held by foreign auto companies? Could anybody believe that General Motors might go bankrupt? Could anyone believe that Ford could lose $12.7 billion in a year? What the auto companies are doing in this environment today to try to survive is what they should have been doing at least 10 years ago, except then some in the industry still felt they knew all the answers.

Airlines offer another example of an industry that faces a crisis, though many people there thought they knew all the answers while being in a state of denial. Airlines such as U.S. Airways, United, and Delta have filed for bankruptcy, and many others are steeply discounting fares in a price war against low-cost and efficient carriers such as Southwest and JetBlue. Once-fabled names such as Pan Am and Braniff International Airlines have already fallen by the wayside. The reality is that executives in the airline industry, as well as unions, are loath to recognize that there is too much capacity in the industry, and that the only viable, though painful, solution might be to let some companies go away and not come back. In the pre-regulation era, airlines could operate profitably even if they operated at 50% capacity. That is no longer possible. According to one assessment, "When deregulation began in 1979, consumers benefited from lower fares, but the airlines never managed to overcome the liability of high fixed costs set during that earlier era."[3] Not recognizing reality makes it difficult to drive through the changes that are needed to transform the industry. As in the auto industry, airline leaders were in denial and waited too long to take the kind of decisive measures that could have saved some of them from the crisis they now face. Whether the trend toward mergers will rescue some of the giants is still to be determined.

Dealing with such denial is one of the toughest challenges for the person trying to lead a company out of a crisis. Ian Bell, one of my former colleagues in the Canadian firm of Touche Ross, was a trustee in bankruptcy proceedings in several situations. He often said his most difficult challenge was getting everybody's attention in bankrupt organizations, and making them realize that they were facing a serious situation, that he was in charge, and that things were going to start happening.

One time, he walked into a construction company that had declared bankruptcy, and the owner asked him who he was. "I am the person who is going to administer this bankruptcy," Bell replied. The company owner said, "Well, we won't really need you because I am sure that it's just a matter of a short time before we are back on our feet. We aren't really going bankrupt at all, so go to the back room if you need to be here. There's a small office there that you can use, even though you won't have much to do."

Bell looked the owner directly in the eye and asked, "Whose Rolls-Royce is that out in the parking lot?" The man said, "Well, that's mine." Bell asked if its title was in the company's name, and the owner said, "Yes." Bell said, "Give me the keys," and when the owner protested, Bell said, "I don't seem to have your attention yet. I am going to liquidate this company for the most I can get in the shortest time possible. Because it is an asset of the company, the Rolls will be the first to go." That was when, for the first time, the owner knew it was a new day, and that things were going to start happening.

Why is denial in the face of crisis so widespread? A possible explanation comes from Robert E. Mittelstaedt, Jr., dean of the W.P. Carey School of Business at Arizona State University and former vice dean of executive education at Wharton. In a recent book, he notes that what finally emerges as a crisis begins as a series of smaller errors that are overlooked. "Enron, WorldCom, and

HealthSouth are now widely known as major business disasters," he writes. "Enron might even be classified as a major economic disaster given the number of employees, pensions and shareholders affected at Enron and their accountants, Arthur Andersen. As investigations unfolded we learned that none was the result of a single bad decision or action. Each involved a complicated web of mistakes that were unnoticed, dismissed as unimportant, judged as minor or purposely ignored in favor of a high-risk high-payoff gamble."[4] Mittelstaedt says that companies must find ways to break this chain of minor errors before they escalate into a full-blown crisis.

In an interview about his book, Mittelstaedt says: "Many executives don't acknowledge the chain. They see the final mistake and think there wasn't an early warning that they could have noticed. The point...is that there are many places you can intervene, especially if you have designed both processes and structures whose function in internal governance is to catch and investigate mistakes." The process can range from a standardization of operating procedures to a focus on customer service. "Customers may be your most important external sensors in the market," Mittelstaedt says. "Yet a company's marketing/customer service division is often isolated from strategy and finance functions. Consequently, much of that valuable customer data is lost."

Even when an organization recognizes in advance that unforeseen crises might derail them, their leaders can fail to take the right steps in time. I recognize that it's impossible to anticipate every possible crisis, but the very act of thinking about them in advance should give you a head start on dealing with whatever crisis befalls you. The pitfall, if it happens, is not taking action that you may have planned in advance.

I had some experience in planning for crises when I was a board member of Banker's Trust. I suggested to the CEO that we form a small group that could look at potential developments that could pose a serious threat to the bank and what we might do about them. He organized a group of four or five people, including some from outside the bank, and we sat around for half a day and talked about potential risks that the institution might face. We talked about five or six possible scenarios. I remember two vividly. One was, What if the Japanese stock market fell substantially, putting pressure on the banks and financial institutions? Bankers Trust had a very large position in Japan at that time. The second scenario was, What if we had a crisis in the derivatives area? Our primary source of derivative transactions for clients involved counter parties, many of them in foreign countries, and in some cases it was very hard to tell whether they could perform if the need arose. The board was concerned with a number of other matters, and I assumed, after our meeting, that the bank internally followed up on these items from a strategic standpoint and gave additional thought to what would be done if they came about. The drop in the Nikkei did happen. The crisis in derivatives also did come about when Bankers Trust suffered huge losses on its derivatives transactions, leading to lawsuits by clients such as Procter & Gamble and Gibson Greetings. Bankers Trust's reputation was dealt a serious blow, and new management headed by Frank Newman did little to stem the slide toward disaster. Eventually, Bankers Trust was taken over by Deutsche Bank in November 1998 for nearly $10 billion. In my view, part of the reason why Bankers Trust, an American banking icon, failed was the leadership's failure to deal effectively with the crisis.

Another pitfall leaders stumble over is simply reacting too slowly to an unfolding crisis that they know exists. The late Lawrence G. Rawl, who was chairman and CEO of Exxon during the Exxon Valdez oil spill, had worked for Exxon for 39 years and was the company's chairman and CEO between 1987 and 1993. But all the good he did while at the company's helm, such as increasing oil reserves, was overshadowed by what was widely perceived to be his failure to deal effectively with the oil-spill crisis.

The facts of the accident are well known. On March 24, 1989, the tanker hit a reef in Prince William Sound in Alaska, causing 11 million gallons of crude oil to leak into the sea. It was one of the country's worst environmental disasters, which polluted more than 1,000 miles of shoreline in addition to affecting birds, marine life, and the livelihood of fishermen along the coast. Still, Exxon did not begin cleaning for two days—and Rawl waited almost three weeks before he visited the site of the spill.

That slowness of response compounded the environmental tragedy and turned into a PR disaster for Exxon. Eventually, Exxon had to buy full-page advertisements in newspapers to apologize for its inaction. By the time the cleanup was completed in 1992, Exxon had spent more than $2 billion dealing with it.

Even when leaders react quickly to crises, they can fail to think through the consequences of the actions they are considering. The crisis at the British Broadcasting Corporation (BBC) in early 2004 is a case in point of small sparks that blew up into a wildfire, eventually leading to the departure of its chairman and director general. A BBC reporter had said in a broadcast that the Blair government "probably knew" that allegations that the Saddam Hussein government in Iraq had weapons of mass destruction were untrue and that the publicly released dossier justifying the war in Iraq had been "sexed up."

The Blair government reacted angrily and demanded an enquiry by a senior judge, Lord Hutton. The reporter's source for the story committed suicide, and the judge's 740-page report on the incident uncovered several errors at the BBC. According to Wharton professor Martin Conyon, the BBC should have handled its crisis better. It should have supported its reporter conditionally until the facts were known. Instead, in defending against the government's attacks, it defended the reporter before the facts were known—and then the leadership had no choice but to step down when the judicial report showed that the BBC had erred.[5]

A Different Approach

I close this chapter on crises with a look at another leader who takes a different approach. Jacob Wallenberg, who belongs to the well-known wealthy Swedish family that has been involved in banking and industry for more than 150 years, sees little difference between leadership during a crisis and the way a leader must operate during so-called normal times. "Sometimes a leader has to lead and point the direction," he says. "But I don't see major differences during normal management and crisis management. In both situations, it is a matter of delegation."

Explaining his approach, Wallenberg notes that in large as well as small organizations, leaders need to put the individual workers in the center. "The more energy you can get out of your employees, the higher will be the quality of work and the better off the employees and the leader will be," he says. To make this arrangement work, says Wallenberg, delegation is crucial. Delegation, in turn, goes hand in hand with accountability. Whether it takes the form of a simple oral agreement or it is a more formal system, "the principle boils down to delegation. You are either capable of delegating or you are not. If you empower other people, you have to de-power yourself. But, if you do it correctly, you empower yourself even more.... You succeed by helping your employees become successful."

In a crisis, delegation is even more critical because "it is important for all individuals to do their jobs" to tackle the crisis, Wallenberg points out. "It's just like a fire exercise. During a crisis, it is more essential than ever for people to be empowered." Wallenberg explains that modern service organizations are essentially flat, and that it simply weakens them if there is an expectation that people will have to keep looking upward to the leader for direction instead of confronting the crisis directly. "The best example of an organization equipped to deal with crises is the modern armed forces," says Wallenberg. "They are dependent on very young people taking tremendous amounts of responsibility in critical situations. They can't be calling home for instructions."

Of course, this raises the question that if an organization should so empower its people, what then is the leader's role during a crisis? According to Wallenberg, it is almost parental—one of providing support and guidance. "You have to stand up and face the crisis—that is very important," Wallenberg says. "Unless you do that, people might lose focus and chaos will ensue."

Summary

- As the leader, remember that you are the person in charge. So you must be the one ultimately to call the shots and be personally involved in the situation.
- Find out the facts as much as possible in the shortest time possible, but you probably don't have time to over-study the situation. Your approach needs to be "Do it, and do it now."
- Execution is critical. If possible, you need to have a follow-up system to see that everyone is doing what they have been told to do and doing it in a timely fashion. Communication is essential, and the key communication needs to be directly with you and not filtered through some third party.
- One of the positive aspects of operating in a crisis is that you're going to find out a good deal about your people that you probably wouldn't be able to find out in any other way.
- You can also use the crisis either during the heat of the battle or after things calm down as a time to make transformational change. You have a burning platform and it enables you not only to accomplish rapidly, but also to get systemic change through the organization that otherwise might be much more difficult to implement.
- We should try to predict crisis. You won't be able to predict all crises, but it's a good idea to sit down and think of the five or six or seven things that could have a major or survival impact on the organization and then discuss the possible consequences, even though they may have a slight probability of happening. It is good to think about what would be done in these situations, and there may be some consequences that are so severe that it would be worthwhile to devise a

plan of action in advance because it might take more time than you have if the crisis actually happens..

- It is probably good to have at least a skeletal crisis team. Although these teams would obviously differ depending on the area, you certainly could have a small group that periodically talks about various potential problems that could arise and understands the general ramifications of crisis management.

- Denial is a major problem that plagues companies that are on their way toward a crisis but fail to recognize the symptoms. Recognize the warning signs well ahead of time, and take corrective steps before the situation escalates into a full-blown crisis.

Endnotes

1 "What Xerox Should Copy and Not Copy from Its Past," *Knowledge@Wharton*, October 25, 2000.

2 These facts and those in the remaining parts of this section are summarized from "The Cow in the Ditch: How Anne Mulcahy Rescued Xerox" and "Crisis Helped to Reshape Xerox in Positive Ways," *Knowledge@Wharton*, November 16, 2005.

3 "Few Survivors Predicted: Why Most Airlines Are Caught in a Tailspin," *Knowledge@Wharton*, February 9, 2005.

4 *Will Your Next Mistake Be Fatal: Avoiding the Chain of Mistakes That Can Destroy Your Organization*, Robert E. Mittelstaedt, Jr. Wharton School Publishing, 2005.

5 "Get Me Rewrite: How the BBC Mishandled Its Own Crisis," *Knowledge@Wharton*, February 25, 2004.

Chapter 6

WHEN ORGANIZATIONS CHANGE: TRANSFORMING THE CULTURE

There are several scenarios in which an organization needs to change. One is when the environment in which it operates has changed while the organization has not, and it is no longer able to function effectively. Another is when an organization has changed over time and become less effective even if its environment hasn't changed. A third is when two organizations are merged and one or, more likely, even both need to change for them to function effectively together.

This chapter describes the problems you will face as a leader when your organization needs to be changed for any reason. A common theme that runs through the chapter is that the organization's culture is most often the biggest obstacle to change.

Since the goal of any transformation is to create a successful organization, this chapter begins by asking what success means to leaders and their constituents. Then the chapter looks at an organization that is faced with a disconnect between its structure, its operating processes, its strategy, and the realities of its environment. The second part examines the special challenges of merging two organizations with differing cultures into one that functions harmoniously and effectively with its environment. The third part describes the potential pitfalls that can undermine the progress of an organization in the process of changing. Finally, I point out what leaders of change should be wary of when they find themselves in other contexts as a part of their primary jobs.

Context: Leading Change in an Organization

One of the principal tasks of leadership is to bring about change in an organization—especially one that has been weakened by neglect, flawed priorities, or failure to respond to a changing business environment.

Success in bringing about change begins with you, the leader. Be prepared for difficult times ahead since leading change is likely to be a hard slog. It is important to remember that failure and adversity are among the key ingredients of success. When people say success is a journey rather than a destination, the underlying idea is that success is merely the ability to withstand the bumps on the way until you achieve your goals. Too often, we view failures and adversity as the absence of success, whereas in reality they are just stations along the way that have to be passed through in order to reach your goals. That is why I believe tenacity and resilience are among the most important attributes of leaders, and never more so than when leading change.

Whenever things get tough, you might draw inspiration—as I do—from Thomas Edison's attitude toward failure and success. When Edison was working on developing an incandescent light bulb, he experimented with hundreds of materials to find the right one for the filament. It was a mind-numbingly tedious and time-consuming exercise. Edison experimented with alloy after alloy—going through a great number of combinations with no results. When his colleagues saw his painstaking efforts, they asked if he was frustrated by these repeated failures. Edison, as the story goes, gave them a puzzled look and asked what failures they were talking about. After all, he had succeeded in finding out that these metals were the wrong material for the bulb. Edison finally found the right material— and also through trial and error created the other systems needed to set up a simple, electricity-based lighting system. The conclusion I draw from this experience is that you fail only if your mind accepts defeat.

I got a lesson in how MBA students view success in their careers when I taught the course in leadership at the Wharton School. In one session I would ask students to say what they would consider success in their own lives. This was a second-year class; the students were busy interviewing with various consulting firms or investment banks, and that issue was at the forefront of their minds. Their responses were essentially that success meant landing a job with McKinsey or Goldman Sachs, and making lots of money. I would then ask them to go home, and for the next class—which was a few days later—imagine that they were at the end of their careers and looking back. From that perspective, what constituted a successful career and life? The answers that came back this time, as you might imagine, were very different. Instead of focusing on finding a prestigious employer who would offer a high salary, the emphasis changed to having a happy family life, giving back to society, being happy with their work, working with people they admired, and achieving their human potential. After reflecting on the real long-term objectives, these factors now become even more important than making money from the long-term perspective.

Most material written on the theory behind leadership points out that the ultimate task of a leader is to help his or her followers attain their ultimate potential. If that happens, not only do individuals attain their own goals, but the organization also benefits to the greatest extent from their contributions. Therefore, it's critical that you understand what success is, in the eyes of the followers, if you are going to bridge their aspirations with yours and cause real change.

It's important to understand that success for you can be very different from success for those whom you lead. Your success will be in changing the organization. Their success may be a combination of things. To understand what these may be, I want to pause here and discuss a study by Korn/Ferry International, the global executive search firm.

In the mid-1980s, the firm conducted a significant study on how executives view success. Carried out in partnership with the UCLA Graduate School of Management, the research project looked at senior executives in America's largest companies and examined various aspects of their careers, in addition to their education, background, and personal data. The 1986 study tracked issues similar to those of a previous landmark study conducted in 1979. I know of no more recent study of this kind, and I believe that their results are still valid today.

Some 42% of the executives that researchers surveyed worked for the industrial sector, while 13% worked in banking and financial services, 8% in insurance, 6% in transportation, and 5% in retail. The remaining 26% of the respondents mainly worked for utilities, energy companies, or technology firms. More than 70% of the respondents had worked for three companies or fewer during their careers—executives had worked for an average of nearly 17 years for their current employer.

How did these executives view success? The most frequently mentioned reasons are illuminating. Many of them—28% of the respondents—defined it as enjoying their work, while 25% viewed it as the ability to effect change. "These were followed by position (13%), controlling the environment (12%) and power (10%). Money was mentioned as an important criterion only 8% of the time," the researchers found (percentages don't add up to 100% because not all reasons given are included).[1]

When asked about traits that enhance success, the respondents overwhelmingly named integrity (71%), concern for results (57%), and desire for responsibility (50%) as the three most important factors. The researchers noted that this ranking represented a shift from their earlier study in 1979, when the executives had ranked concern for results as the most important driver of success. Interestingly, respondents to the 1986 survey also placed less value on creativity or aggressiveness as traits that enhanced success, unlike their predecessors in the 1970s.

The last question in the survey asked the respondents to identify the single most important factor that contributed to their success. The executives identified hard work as the number-one factor, along with others such as ambition, luck, effective execution, perseverance, and interpersonal skills, among others. A large number of executives also said success depends on "willingness to take risks, ability to motivate people, self-confidence, leadership, being a self-starter, adaptability and careful planning."

Although these may have been the views of top executives during the 1980s and are still relevant, they have shifted somewhat after the dot-com boom and bust of the 1990s. In 2000, Korn/Ferry International conducted a study in collaboration with London Business School, titled "Tomorrow's Leaders Today: Career Aspirations and Motivations," which clearly showed the shift in thinking. This time, the Korn/Ferry and LBS study found that the "new lifestyles made possible by the Internet" led to a major shift in power between employers and employees. "Most importantly, the executives themselves have changed," the researchers wrote. "Whether in a start-up or established, mature business, through years of downsizing and restructuring, employee loyalty is a thing of the past." As one executive, who defected from a traditional consulting firm, put it, "I think the loyalty's gone, and it's all about opportunity."[2]

Another major shift in the way executives saw their careers in the 21st century was the tremendous emphasis they placed on independence. "Today's high-performing executives are most influenced by the quest for two forms of independence," the study said. The first is independence at work, which the executives defined as "control over their own projects, the freedom to schedule and prioritize their own work—and to be rewarded accordingly." The second is independence from work, which they viewed as "a better balance of work and private life, less attachment to the office location and more time for themselves."

Based on its findings, the researchers concluded that companies face a major challenge today because the work ethos has "changed entirely from being company-facing to market-facing." In other words, the development goals of high-performing executives have changed from increasing their potential value to the company to increasing their future market potential. "They want to be entrepreneurs—interacting with the market—not bureaucrats finding their way around an organization. They want training and developmental input from an external perspective, not just from a mentor who will speak primarily from an internal viewpoint."

Don't be disturbed by the new 21st-century attitude cited in the Korn/Ferry study. It fits right in with what I have been saying throughout this book—beginning in the first chapter: Find out the needs and desires and goals of the followers and help them attain those goals, maximize their human potential, and bridge their goals to yours. Losing sight of what success means to those you would lead can cause leaders to go down the wrong roads.

How Leaders Transform Organizations

In the ultimate analysis, success in leading transformations over the long run depends on the leader's vision in developing a strategic plan. Based largely on my experience of bringing about change at Touche Ross and the Wharton School, I believe that any leader who is serious about transforming an organization should consider the process I describe next. This may not be the only way to bring about organizational transformation but it worked for me. At least it's a starting point for you to move toward your own method of transformation.

1. **Listen a lot.** Before you can change an organization, you must understand its reality in as much depth as possible. To do that, you first need to do a lot of listening. Even before I formally took over as the Dean at Wharton, I spent countless hours listening to faculty, staff, and students at the school—and that helped me to understand the totality of the school's situation.

2. **Formulate your strategic plan.** After you have heard what others have to say, you then must digest the information you have collected and formulate a strategic plan. In formulating the plan, even if you have lots of ideas in your mind already, meet regularly with your core leadership team and go over the plan in a collegial fashion. Not only will that result in a better plan, but it also will ensure that the team is committed to it. After the plan is written down, it can be implemented and milestones toward its achievement can be tracked. This is not a step to be delegated to some internal or external planning expert. They can help you with the details later.

3. **Make sure you have the right team to implement the plan.** It's very likely that you won't find everyone willing to get onboard with change no matter what you do. So you have to bring in some new people. Every tired, complacent person must be replaced with innovative, flexible people who have some new ideas. This enables the leader to build a team that he or she can count on. The hard truth—and one that is very difficult for some high-profile CEOs to swallow— is that leaders are almost never as much in charge as others (and they themselves) think they are, and if they don't have key lieutenants to execute the plan, forget it.

   And remember, when you are transforming things, it won't happen because you send out a memo with a proclamation, nor will it happen primarily because you have all these smart people at the executive office writing a manual on what to do and how to do it. Transformation is executed where the rubber meets the road—with the line managers. As a leader, you should spend more time with them, mentor them, and, if they get the job done, pay them very well— better than most in the Corporate office.

4. **Communicate constantly.** It is not enough to have a plan that is written down and sitting on people's bookshelves.

If you want it to succeed, you must communicate about it constantly so that everyone at each level of the organization is clear about the plan.

5. **Align individual goals with the objectives of the strategic plan.** The strategic plan will remain a meaningless exercise to most people unless it touches them personally. As a leader, you need to ensure that compensation, promotions, and other incentives are tied to success in achieving milestones set out in the strategic plan. This implies that decision making needs to be pushed down the ranks. Making decisions at the top about issues that should be decided down the line can be dangerous. If the organization has to wait for the CEO to make every decision before it can move ahead, it is in real trouble. Any organization in which a micromanager has to be involved in everything will be limited to that manager's capacity of time and ability to make timely decisions. Of course, you have to be involved in the most important strategic decisions, but day-to-day, operating decisions must be made by a large number of people who feel empowered to make them. People at all levels in an organization must understand that they have not only the authority but also the responsibility to make decisions.

All this won't work unless you are able to mobilize everyone—especially key managers—around your strategy. And this depends on understanding one of the principles of leadership I described in the first chapter: *A leader mobilizes followers by finding out their goals, desires, wants, and needs, and makes them believe that the leader is truly trying to help them achieve these aspirations. At the same time, in order to achieve the goals of the organization, the leader must bridge the individual goals of the followers and the overall goals that are incorporated in, for example, a strategic plan.*

6. **Measure your performance against the plan.** How will you know whether you are on track? You need to constantly

measure how the organization is performing against the metrics you have defined. It often helps if an external group is involved with such tracking so that you have an objective view and not a rosy picture that insiders in a specific area want to believe in and portray to make themselves look successful. At Wharton, after we had decided that our strategic plan would consist of goals such as hiring top faculty members, increasing fundraising, strengthening the curriculum, and so forth, and reduced these to measurable metrics, we constantly monitored and communicated where we stood in relation to our plan.

7. **Modify your plan as you go along.** Even the best-laid strategic plans cannot predict how things will work in the future. New opportunities may come your way, and some that seemed promising in concept may bomb when you try to implement them. When that happens, adhering blindly to a blueprint won't help. Your plan must be flexible and dynamic enough to let you make tactical changes even as you continue to pursue your strategy.

8. **If you hit obstacles, don't hesitate to send a message to the organization.** Organizational inertia is a reality. There will probably be some unit leaders who will not buy into the plan or who will continuously make excuses as to why they aren't meeting their goals. They are stonewalling you, hoping the program will go away or, better yet, that you will go away. If that happens, don't shy away from confrontation—it is essential in the interests of the organization as a whole. Fire those unit leaders—you probably didn't think they were that good anyway. They led in a negative fashion, saying they were protecting their division from crazy ideas and problems from the executive office and top leadership. At the same time, promote those people in other divisions who are doing a great job. Let everyone know how serious you are about the plan.

9. **Celebrate the achievement of each milestone.**
   Publicly praise and reward people who help the strategic
   plan succeed. That is how you will be able to build momentum and keep up everyone's energy along the way.

A Tale of Three Transformations

Now that we have discussed the steps needed to bring about organizational change, let's look at the experiences of three leaders of
change and see how they match up with what I have been saying.
Gordon Bethune demonstrated his leadership skills in turning
around the culture at Continental Airlines after he arrived from
Boeing as CEO in 1994.[3] He said the airline was "going nowhere
fast." It had all the problems that could possibly plague an organization whose job was to take people and their belongings from place
to place safely and on time. Judged by quality measures such as
"flight arrivals within 15 minutes of schedule" or "lost luggage,"
Continental was "dead last" and the "worst" among the top 10
airlines in the U.S. Understandably, its customers were deeply
unhappy. According to Bethune, in 1994 Continental had almost
"three times as many complaints as the industry average."

The main reason Continental got into this predicament was
that the previous leadership had cut costs too deeply. Bethune
knew that it costs money to run an airline properly, but expenses
at Continental had been slashed so much that it was no longer
possible to run an efficient operation and the company was losing
business. "You can make a pizza so cheap that no one will eat it,
and you can run an airline so cheap that no one will fly it," he
says. "Cutting costs beyond a point just doesn't work."

Bethune decided that it was important to focus on the underlying cause of the problem rather than its superficial manifesta-
tions. "It's like a patient who goes to a doctor's office complaining
about a swelling in the leg," he says. "The doctor checks the blood
pressure. If that is what is causing the problem, he has to treat the
blood pressure before he can cure the swelling."

He also knew that success would depend on his being able to articulate a clear and convincing strategy to his workers.

Four-Point Go Forward Plan

First, Bethune knew that the airline's most important priority was to get its passengers to their destinations on time. As he puts it, "We needed a product strategy that worked consistently for our customers. In meetings with employees, I would hold up a wristwatch and say, 'This watch has to work every day, 365 days a year, and it has be completely reliable. That is how a customer measures its value.' Continental has to be just as reliable in getting customers where they want to go."

Second, Bethune argued that Continental needed an effective market strategy. This involved figuring out which destinations the airline should fly to and at what prices. "Developing the market strategy involves allocating the product and pricing it," Bethune explains. "You need to compete where you can win."

Third, Continental needed a financial strategy to make sure that it had the capital and the liquidity to run the airline's operations. "We needed the right capital structure. It's like having oxygen in your lungs."

The fourth element of Bethune's strategy—and possibly the most important—was the people strategy. The product, market, and capital strategies would not work if Continental Airlines' employees did not throw their weight behind the plan to turn around the airline. "We had to get the confidence and focus of the employees, and we needed to work on all four fronts simultaneously," Bethune says.

Each of these four elements was given a catchy name and the plan was called the "Four-Point Go Forward Plan." These were the four points:

- Fly To Win (market strategy)
- Fund the Future (financial strategy)

- Make Reliability a Reality (product strategy)
- Working Together (people strategy)

The People Strategy

Of the four parts of the strategy, Bethune knew that the fourth was key to changing the culture. The company's 40,000 employees needed to pull in the same direction. The problem was that after going through several CEOs, each of whom had his or her own pet theories of what was wrong and how to fix it, the employees were cynical and morale was low. As he put it, "We could have had the perfect plan, but if the implementation was messed up, it would never have worked." "Most failures are caused when implementation fails. Just because you are the CEO, that does not mean the employees are going to bust their butts for you. I own the lake where I fish, but I still need bait. If you want employees to implement the plan, you need to show appreciation."

Bethune developed a simple plan to demonstrate employee appreciation. He announced that each time Continental was among the top five airlines in the country in terms of flights being on time, all employees would get a bonus. Continental came up with the bonus amount through a basic calculation. It cost the airline an additional $5 million a month when flights were late; if they were on time, Bethune figured that half that money—$2.5 million, or $65 per person—should go to the employees. While the amount was not large, it had tremendous symbolic value—it indicated that the company recognized and was willing to reward the employees for their success. "It was a nice little thank you for employees," says Bethune. The plan worked. By March 1995— only one year after he arrived—Continental had become that number-one airline in the country for on-time flights.

Bethune also put in place a profit-sharing plan under which 20% of pretax income would go to the employees. Continental's shareholders viewed success differently than its customers. For shareholders, the primary measure of success was profitability. Bethune shrewdly recognized that even if a flight took off and landed on time, employees often preferred a partially full flight over a full one because it meant less work for them. If the employees knew, however, that they would receive part of the profits, they would make sure that every flight had as many passengers as it could hold. "If I share my profits with you, you won't resent the fact that you have to work harder for the customers," Bethune says. "The employees win when the customers win. As a result, all the employees knew they were in the same boat as the customers. When one won, they all won. We acted as a team. We beat the competition, not each other. We had 40,000 people all pulling in the same direction."

Again, the plan worked—in July 1995 Continental Airlines announced the largest quarterly profit in its history and it ended the year with profits of $225 million, the largest annual profit the airline had made in its 61-year history.

Lessons from Continental's Turnaround

What leadership lessons can be learned from the way Gordon Bethune turned around Continental Airlines? When asked this question, he explains that "there is a correlation between employee satisfaction and business success. If you are the leader, you have to give this issue time and energy. You can't depend on your HR department to figure this out. You have to do it yourself."

Bethune also believes that constant communication with employees was crucial to his success at Continental. "Before a football game, everyone goes into a huddle," he says. "And it's everyone, not just part of the team. In employee meetings I would hold up a wristwatch and say, 'Which part of this watch don't you need?' We needed everyone and communicated with everyone. Every Friday, I'd put out a three- to five-minute voice mail about how Continental was doing. Every employee got it. Another rule I followed was to never lie. You don't lie to your doctor, you don't lie to your attorney, and you don't lie to your employees. These are the fundamentals that helped turn around Continental."

Bethune says that leaders need more than just marketing and financial strategies to succeed. "Most of your success depends on your reliability and the trust you inspire in people. You trust that your mother loves you—even if she is sometimes mad at you. That is what makes motherhood reliable and gives it its value. If you are running an airline, people must be able to rely on you. You must earn that trust to succeed as a leader. Sometimes I am asked, 'How come you know so much about people?' I say, 'I used to be one.'"

Larry Bossidy, whom we met in Chapter 1, "Leadership Principles: The Basis of Successful Leadership," and again in Chapter 3, "The Top-Down Organization: Learning That It's Not So Simple," is a leader whose experience in leading organizational change sheds light on how to lead an organization through change. Causing change in an organization sometimes requires a radical departure in direction, but at other times it simply involves doing what you are supposed to be doing anyway. That is what Larry Bossidy found when he left General Electric in mid-1991, where he had been the chief operating officer of GE Credit, to join AlliedSignal, now renamed Honeywell after the two companies merged in December 1999.

Earlier we saw that Bossidy believes that for leaders to succeed, they have to be good at three things. As he puts it, "You have to be good at strategy, you have to be good with people, and you have to be good in operations." When he got to AlliedSignal's headquarters in Morristown, New Jersey, he was appalled. We saw Bossidy's pungent comments about the situation in Chapter 3, and they bear repeating here. "Allied Signal had all three processes," he says. "They had a strategic plan; they had a people appraisal process; and they had an operating plan or budget—but they were all done about one inch deep. They had not taken them on in the depth that was required." What was lacking was the ability to execute their strategy. The theme of execution has become Bossidy's mantra and he believes execution is a direct responsibility of the CEO.

As he explains it, the buck truly stops with the leader. "If leadership is action-oriented and holds itself accountable, ultimately that will bring about a very positive culture. If, on the other hand, it is lax and its goals are not articulated clearly and people are always excusing their inability to perform, that infiltrates a culture in a negative way," he says.

Bossidy says a colleague told him something about culture that he wished he had learned earlier in his career. "He told me that our culture is a summation of our acts...not our pronouncements, or what other people want us to be, but a summation of what we do," he says.

Marsha Evans, whose leadership during crises I described in Chapter 5, "The Organization in Crisis: Turning Danger into Opportunity," is a former president of the Red Cross, and faced difficult times bringing about a change in the cultures of the Navy and Girl Scouts before she became president of the Red Cross. In the Navy, where she rose to the rank of Admiral, she says, "My assignments were never more than two years long. If you are on the promotion track, you can never stay too long in the same assignment; you have to get to the next one up the rung. In the Navy we talked about culture change, but we didn't have the time to do much about it because we just moved on."

"My first experience in being in an organization longer than two-and-a-half years was when I joined the Girl Scouts as president. There, we had to work hard to modernize and improve the sense of urgency and the processes in a very conservative and change-averse organization. It can be done."

How did Evans bring about change in the Girl Scouts and, later, in the Red Cross? "In both organizations it was very helpful to have a strong founder foundation," she says. Girl Scouts was founded by Juliette Gordon Low in 1912, and Clara Barton founded the American Red Cross in 1881. "In both cases, it was very helpful to have a rich history. My constant refrain was, 'How do we preserve and protect the vision of the founder but make it relevant for today and even more relevant for tomorrow?' It helps to have that really strong anchor."

According to Evans, bringing about organizational transformation requires the leader to create what she calls "the burning platform for change" in the minds of people—at multiple levels of leadership within the organization, as well as donors, volunteers, and other supporters. "How do you create the burning platform for change?" she asks. "How do you create the necessity of doing things differently? That is really the hard question."

Evans says it does not help to take the imperious approach—"I want to change something because I have decided I want to change something." Leaders who try that approach are unlikely to get very far—especially in a nonprofit organization. "Trying to change an organization requires creating a burning platform for change, or you are going to get passive aggressive resistance at all levels," Evans says. "When you want to bring about change, about 20% of the people will climb onboard with you right away, and they want to be ahead of you in the change. About 60% will come along if you convince them. And about 20% will hang back and may try to subvert the change. The important thing is to help that last group of people transition into some other setting. Frankly, I helped people transition out. In some cases, I waited too long to do that."

While Evans was preparing to bring about these changes at the Girl Scouts and Red Cross, she tried to understand both organizations as much as she could. She also made every effort not to rush things and to build as much consensus as possible around the key issues. "In both the Girl Scouts and the Red Cross, people asked me, 'What is your program going to be?'" she says. "There is a kind of delicacy about putting people off until you can understand the organization. It takes a little while to get to know the organization and understand the urgent priorities, until you can get the leverage to change the organization. It also takes time to get the right people you want on your team. That takes a lot of time. The big challenge for me was fending off the questioner who somehow expected that in the first 30 days I would have a fully formed plan. I understood that they were hungry for direction, but I couldn't do it in 30 days. My continuing refrain was that we are going to take this slowly so that we can get it right from the start. I am a believer in the 'go slow to go fast' school. If you take time to plan properly upfront, then the change will unroll much more smoothly. I have an aversion to the idea that this is my plan. I want a plan that we have created—and that is going to guide all of us as we go forward. I just happen to be the person who is accountable for it."

In her effort to change the American Red Cross culture, Evans drew up a strategic plan. One of her guiding principles was to ask what Clara Barton, founder of the American Red Cross, might have done if she were alive. "A little-known part of the history of Clara Barton is that that woman was a brutal driver," says Evans. "She just would not give up. Her image is that of a person with a divine countenance, but the real Clara Barton was a tough leader. If she were here today, she would be moving us faster in the direction of modernization and change...."

"So we started on a strategic planning process that involved the participation of 6,000 people," Evans continues. "We had focus groups, used e-tools, etc. I could have written the plan myself with help from a couple of good writers, but the process of engaging with thousands of people including all the chapters and volunteers was very important. Of course, it took more time to do it this way—we started in October and ended in May. That process in some ways was more important, frankly, than the content. Many people who got involved in the plan and helped to shape it began to own it, and then it was their plan. In any organization there are people who like to hang back and criticize, and certainly we have those too in the Red Cross; but by and large, the leadership of the organization at all levels engaged. It [was] huge, in terms of people knowing that they counted and they would be heard."

In the end, Marsha Evans resigned in late 2005 as the president of the Red Cross following conflicts with the organization's board. Her experience at both the Girl Scouts and the Red Cross taught her a good deal about the challenges of transforming nonprofits. In an interview before her resignation, she explained that the Red Cross suffers from "a lot of the ills of volunteer organizations," such as the existence of volunteer empires combined with a conservative, risk-averse culture. Though she successfully managed the cultural change in the organization, she could not completely win over the board.

Bethune, Bossidy, and Evans emphasize the importance of having a strategic plan that the organization buys into. Without that commitment from the organization, the best strategic plan in the world will go nowhere.

Mergers and Organizational Change

When two organizations merge—or one acquires another—it is almost certain that a change in culture will have to take place for the combined organizations to succeed.

There are various reasons that can impel two organizations to join together. One organization might be visibly in deep trouble, and it sets out to find an appropriate partner for a merger to solve the problems. Sometimes such mergers might work but more often they do not work as well as they should. I will discuss some of the reasons for failure shortly.

First, however, I will assert that the same factors that determine success in changing a single organizational culture apply equally to a merger of two organizations. Cultural change is inevitable. But, perhaps counter-intuitively, the best culture change is not for one organization to adopt the culture of the other. To succeed over the long term, the two organizations must find a new culture that will enable them to realize the strengths that each brings to the merger.

I agree with Dennis C. Cary and Dayton Ogden, of consulting firm Spencer Stuart, when they say in their book *The Human Side of M&A: How CEOs Leverage the Most Important Asset in Deal Making,* "Our thesis, which is reinforced throughout this book, is that scrutinizing the financial side of [mergers] is only half of the equation, and is hardly an assurance of success...we discuss why it is advisable to have a thorough evaluation of management teams and prevailing cultures before, during, and after a merger." They go on to argue, "It will be important to identify players in the companies who are wedded to the old way of doing things and would likely be roadblocks to the creation of a *new vision and a new culture*" (emphasis added).

Once whoever leads the merged organization realizes the need to find a new vision and create a new culture, the actual process of change should follow what I have described previously for change in a single organization. There is really no significant difference between the two situations.

I would add that a complicating factor in making a merger successful and creating a new culture is the fact that in my experience, there is always a winner and loser. I have been on 14 New York Stock Exchange boards, and during the 25 years that I have been active as a board member I have been involved in a great number of mergers. Also, in my experience I have been involved with a considerable number of mergers that were billed as "mergers of equals." There is no such thing as a merger of equals. Somebody always wins out. Throughout the organization, you can be sure that, at least subconsciously, everyone is hoping their side wins because they don't know what it means to them if the "merger of equals" idea prevails. After a time you start seeing people leave for one reason or another, and the balance always seems to be tipped to one side or the other. The leader must see that the best person is in the various jobs no matter which background they came from. Only the unsure leader wants his own former people around because he knows they are "loyal." It will take heavy emphasis and pressure from the top to ensure that the company ends up much better off because when you put groups of people from two organizations together, you must choose the best from among the candidates for each job and not decide on the basis of political connections, friendships, seniority, or other irrelevant reasons. If the leader doesn't stay involved, the job's not going to get done, and the warfare down in the trenches to see who wins out will be detrimental to creating a new culture, getting daily business done, preventing a loss of morale, and moving forward with the best talent.

Next I point out the potential pitfalls awaiting leaders who would change cultures, including those in merged organizations.

Potential Pitfalls in Leading Change

One of the most common mistakes that many egotistical leaders make is that they think they can do everything themselves. The hard truth—and one that is very difficult for high-profile CEOs to swallow—is that leaders are almost never as much in charge as others (and they themselves) think they are.

Newspapers often write about how the CEO of a certain company did this and the CEO of another company did that. Chances are the most the CEO ever did was to okay a decision—if he or she even did that. The CEOs seem to be responsible for whatever happens in the organization—good or bad. What about the other people in the organization? You can be sure of one thing: Lee Iacocca did not design the Mustang, and Steve Jobs personally did not sit down and think up the iPod. Still, it is usually the CEO who gets (and often takes) the credit for these successes.

When an organization fails, though, it is harder to believe that the leader should not accept the responsibility. Is it really believable that Jeff Skilling, who went on trial for criminal fraud in January 2006 for the collapse of Enron after participating in one of the most sweeping changes of culture in recent history, did not know what was going on at the Houston-based energy company?

Whatever his defense attorneys might argue, common sense tells us that when a company conceals enormous amounts of debt by moving them into off-balance sheet entities and presents a distorted view of the company's financial health, it cannot sustain this false picture forever. Sooner or later the house of cards is bound to come tumbling down, as it did when Enron went bankrupt at the end of 2001. Skilling must have known what was going on, even if his lawyers now argue that he was misled by subordinates such as Andrew Fastow, Enron's former CFO, who pleaded guilty. After the trial ended, Skilling was found guilty of 19 of the 28 counts of fraud, conspiracy, insider trading, and lying to auditors; he was sentenced to 24 years in prison. Fastow pleaded guilty and was sentenced to 6 years; in early 2007 he was serving his sentence in Louisiana.

Even the wise leader who delegates parts of a transformation to trusted subordinates must watch out for "bush sitters." This is my term for a lot of people who are out there who can impact the execution of plans of the leader. These people sit in the bushes all day long and are somewhat invisible because that is essentially all they do. But when the leader makes a decision in the organization and takes the entity in a new direction, for instance, they come halfway out of the bushes and say, "I don't think you're right. You're making a mistake. You shouldn't do that." And then they go back into the bushes. The leader who is making decisions, taking risks, trying new things will inevitably make a bad decision along the way. When this happens, the bush sitter stands up as tall as possible and says, "I told you so."

Bush sitters can be detrimental to an organization and the leader's plans. They can cause doubts in the organization, they can make people lose confidence, and sometimes they can even cause people to question the abilities of the leader. They are generally malcontents, though they are often quite good at their specific area of endeavor. First you try to ignore them, and if they become too detrimental to the organization, you get rid of them. I don't think that totally takes care of the problem because they will be replaced by others and there will always be some around. Just keep moving ahead. Change is not going to happen if you are not willing to try new directions and take risks, and you may have to tolerate some "bush sitters" along the way as you find ways of minimizing their effect.

I've always liked Theodore Roosevelt's view of those who take risks in the pursuit of change. You probably have heard this quote before, but it might be appropriate to read it in the context of this chapter. He said, "It is not the critic who counts; not the man who points out how the strong one stumbles, or where the doer of deeds could have done them better. The credit belongs to the person who is actually in the arena, whose face is marred by dust and sweat and blood; who strives valiantly; who errs and comes short again and again; because there is not effort without error and shortcoming; but who does actually strive to do the deeds." Roosevelt went on to praise the person who "knows the great enthusiasms, the great devotions; who spends themselves in a worthy cause; who at best knows in the end the triumphs of high achievement and who at the worst, if they fail, at least fail while daring greatly, so that their place shall never be with those cold timid souls who know neither victory nor defeat."

A particularly treacherous pitfall for leaders of change is to fail to balance short-term goals for the organization with long-term goals. Leaders who can continuously turn out quarterly earnings increases without building the organization to its greatest long-term potential may be in for a rude awakening. The shareholders and the board might find that their haste in congratulating management on its quarterly performance was premature—and that no value has been built for the long term. An organization can end up as an empty shell at the end of the trip. This is a major problem in business today. Stock analysts drive the quest for quarterly earnings and create a guidance mentality that is lethal. It is the main reason several companies went down the road (slowly at first) of cooking the books in the 1980s and 1990s. At the beginning they just needed a couple of pennies to make the quarterly earnings forecast, and then it escalated from there. Now we have a whole new breed of people who are causing short-term thinking, such as the hedge funds, who team up to lean on the company for short-term stock appreciation all in the name of shareholder value, buy lots of stock back, pay out dividends, take on debt. Growth, new products, research, training people...what do these do for us? Nothing—unless they result in short-term profits, or so their argument seems to go.

Short-term thinking can also lead to losing sight of the customer when failing to create long-term value. This can easily happen in today's world of large corporations, where there are multiple layers of managers and ensconced bureaucracies. They can forget that the customer pays the rent and the salaries and that without customers there is no ongoing business. I know of many organizations that are not commercial in nature, and they think they have no customers. My initial experience as dean at the Wharton School—described in Chapter 8, "The Academic Organization: Learning from the Wharton Experience"—made it clear that many of the faculty and administration thought that they had no customers when, in fact, students were their most important customers, and the companies that hired them were almost as important.

I promised to discuss the pitfalls of mergers, and I begin by asking, Why do so many mergers fail? I believe that happens for at least two reasons. First, when two weak organizations come together, they do not necessarily make a strong one; it may result in a large, weak organization. Second, mergers also fail because to succeed in a merger requires a cultural change, but that is rarely easy. If a company has been run since its inception by engineers, it may not be easy to transform it into an entrepreneurial organization. If it has been run by accountants, it is a steep hill to turn it quickly into a marketing organization. If employees have always waited for orders to be received on what to do, it's hard to empower them to make decisions for their area of responsibility.

Consider, for example, the merger of Hewlett Packard (HP) with Compaq Computer, which was aimed at strengthening the

Palo-Alto, California, company and helping it compete with its two major competitors in desktop and laptop computers, Dell and IBM. The day that Carleton (Carly) Fiorina, then chairman and CEO of HP, announced the merger in September 2001, the stock price declined to $18.87 from $23.21 the previous trading day. After a bitter shareholder battle that lasted years, Fiorina eventually left the company in February 2005, thanks in part to the failed merger. Part of the problem was that the two companies did not see the kind of cultural change that is needed to make a merger successful. Conflicting cultures and failure to integrate are probably the major cause of failed mergers, after the problem of a bad merger that shouldn't have been made in the first place. To transform a corporate culture, as I said before, you have to bring in some new people. This is what Fiorina failed to do.

Under its new CEO, Mark V. Hurd, the company is now in a period of transition and consolidation. Its revenue has increased but its earnings have not kept pace. Only time will tell whether the initial decision to merge with Compaq can be saved through better leadership—though in early 2007 the company's fortunes seemed to be shining; it overtook Dell to become the world's largest PC company. Still, its missteps during the merger offer a cautionary example of what can go wrong in a merger.

Leading in Other Contexts

While Larry Bossidy was leading change at AlliedSignal, he also served on the Business Council and Business Roundtable. As a dynamic leader, he realized that he needed to adopt a different style when he sought to influence the culture among his equally distinguished and accomplished peers if they were to accomplish anything worthwhile. I can do no better than quote what he said in the first chapter of this book: "What is good for the goose isn't always good for the gander. In other words, if you have CEOs around the table, depending on the business they operate, they might take relatively pedestrian positions that benefit their own companies. You can't blame them for that. I've done this, as a matter of fact. However, you might say something like, "This business round-table has as one of its goals to influence legislation. And if the legislation we are considering goes the way it's being proposed, it will certainly have an effect on business. It may not have an effect on your business, or it may have a slightly positive effect on your business. But in the general interest of the round-table, it will have an overall detrimental effect." So you appeal to their sense of logic and decency. At the end of the day, you don't automatically command all those votes unanimously, but you still make a recommendation for what should be done for the majority of those on the round-table."

To put it another way, you will probably have to rein in your impulse to take charge of a peer group.

Summary

- Make sure you listen a lot. Most of the problems and answers are already out there.
- Develop your strategic plan. Get your own arms around it and then "collegially" make it better—sign up people along the way.
- Be sure you have the right people. Assess your team, then get some new ones, promote some, get rid of some. Don't wait.
- Communicate, communicate. You simply have to do this all the time to keep the plan in the forefront of the organization.
- Align the goals of your people with the plan. Tie elements of the strategic plan directly to compensation, promotion, and so on.
- Identify major measurement requirements and tools. You need to track how your plan is progressing.
- Measure, measure. Unless you measure, you will not know how near or far from your plan you are.

- Fine-tune your plan as you go. Don't get stuck on a plan that's going off track. Be prepared to make mid-course corrections.
- If necessary, send a message to the organization. They may not have fully understood your vision.
- Hold some celebrations along the way. Nothing will galvanize your people like recognizing their contributions to a plan that's working.
- Don't just praise, reward. Tie compensation to performance. Those who make the plan a success should be paid well—often better than those in the executive suite.

Endnotes

1 Korn/Ferry *International's Executive Profile: A Survey of Corporate Leaders in the Eighties.*

2 Korn/Ferry *International: Tomorrow's Leaders Today* (2000).

3 Gordon Bethune describes his experience in more detail in his remarkable book, *From Worst to First: Behind the Scenes of Continental's Remarkable Comeback* (paper edition, Wiley 1999).

Chapter 7

THE ENTREPRENEURIAL ORGANIZATION: SHARING YOUR VISION WITH OTHERS

Entrepreneurial leadership poses special challenges. Entrepreneurs are in a unique situation—they are generally alone. The entrepreneur may have investors or advisors, but in the end the entrepreneur is the decision maker, and often decisions need to be made quickly, making it possible for entrepreneurs to execute rapidly. That is why entrepreneurial environments provide fertile ground for leadership.

Although entrepreneurship might not at first appear to be a context in its own right—like academia or a professional services organization—starting or leading an entrepreneurial venture has its own unique challenges. Building an organization as an entrepreneur calls for specific leadership skills—including the ability to identify the right business opportunities, finding ways to judge the right level of resources that should be invested to turn the opportunity into a profitable investment, and finding the right CEO and leadership team to make that happen.

In this chapter, I describe how leadership in this context works differently than in other contexts I explore in the book. Most of the chapter is about my experience as an entrepreneur after I left the deanship at the Wharton School in 1990. I share with you the hard-won lessons that I learned that can increase your chances for success as an entrepreneurial leader.

First I explain how I came to be an entrepreneur. The rest of the chapter is in reverse chronological order. I describe the entrepreneurial ventures that went well from the beginning, though they were not the first that I and my partners embarked on. My intention is to tell you how a well-planned and -researched venture should be led. Then, in keeping with my format of these context chapters, I tell you about the pitfalls you face as an entrepreneurial leader and describe the near disasters that I faced when I first began. In the last section of this chapter, I warn you about leading in a different context—the one that you will find yourself in if your venture is successful.

One final point. This chapter is about an entrepreneur whose motivation was simply to become an entrepreneur. I knew which business I wanted to enter: I wanted to invest in companies that my colleagues and I could build into valuable enterprises—even though I wasn't certain in which industries these companies might be. In that sense my experience differed from that of someone who might venture into an entrepreneurial career without knowing what business to enter, or someone who had an idea for a particular business, or who had an invention to commercialize. Nevertheless, I believe that my experiences would be similar to those of other entrepreneurs no matter what their intentions may be.

Context: The Entrepreneurial Organization

The challenge the entrepreneurial leader faces is knitting together the investors, advisors, customers, and vendors with his or her vision. That is a matter of negotiation. It is the price entrepreneurs must pay for the fact that, though they might be alone in making decisions, they must operate within a business framework to succeed.

To ground this chapter in the real world, I describe my experience after I left the Wharton School.

Life After Wharton

About a year before the end of my seven-year term as dean, I decided it was time to leave Wharton. The faculty offered me a second term, but I firmly believe—as I have stated elsewhere—that no one should be in the same job too long. So I decided that it was time to move on. I sat back and thought for a few months about what I might do. I concluded that I probably had one more full-time career left in me, and I said to myself, "I should try to make this the best one yet—last and best."

I thought a lot about what I wanted to do and finally ended up with three bullet points on a piece of paper that were most important in terms of defining this phase of my career:

- Have fun and do something meaningful.
- Do something of excellence that I could be proud of.
- Be successful and make some money.

These three points were written in order of importance. To have fun and do something meaningful was paramount. Then I asked myself what would fit into that category. I decided I did not want to head something that was in effect someone else's business. I also did not want to get into the nonprofit world, because through my dealings with such organizations I had learned that with all their committees and boards, they moved much too slowly for me. I surely did not want to go into politics. Finally I concluded that I needed to set up my own business, to become an entrepreneur. This would give me the flexibility to do what I wanted.

I set up The Palmer Group with offices two blocks from the University of Pennsylvania, and I wasn't exactly sure what I was going to do except that it would certainly be in keeping with the three criteria I had set up. A lot of people suggested that I raise a fund to buy out companies. I definitely did not want to do that. Imagine going to investors to try and raise funding, and when they asked what I intended to do with the money, having to say that my primary goal was "to have fun and do something meaningful." Apart from being a hard sell and not exactly appealing from a business standpoint, it might make investors wonder if I was being serious. No, that wouldn't work. So I decided I would just do this on my own, whatever "this" was. In the end I decided that we would buy small companies, build them up, and probably exit some day, but not in a typical venture capital format. I didn't like the thought of buying a company, building it up, and flipping it. I preferred the approach of acquiring a business, building it up, and looking at it as if we would own it forever, even though some day we might exit.

Our initial venture nearly sank us, and I will describe it and other early experiences later as object lessons on the pitfalls that lie in store for would-be entrepreneurs. As we gained experience, we found a business that held great potential for us: professional schools. It wasn't the only business we entered, but it is a good example of the kind of entrepreneurial leadership that works.

I had a secretary who came with me from Wharton, Sharon Brandt. Unfortunately, her husband was in the Navy and had to move to another city, and she had to leave. (After that I have had two great assistants during the past 15 years—Becky Leonard, followed by Jean Drake. As any leader knows, you can't function without a top assistant.) I had a Wharton student, James Membrino, working for me as an intern and when he graduated he joined us full time. He was very good. We hired Wharton students part time to help us analyze companies we were thinking about acquiring. One thing I remember about most of the graduate students is that they were on the phone looking for jobs for a significant amount of time. After we started acquiring, my son Steve, an attorney, came up from Washington two days a week to help us.

The Professional Schools Business

In 1993, my son Brad, who was also in the entrepreneurial business, uncovered an opportunity with Career Com, a public company in Pennsylvania that had gone bankrupt. The company had operated several schools, including six that deserved to remain open because they were the best of the bunch and had the potential to survive. The business had been horribly mismanaged, and as we went into bankruptcy court to go through the process of acquiring these schools, I realized again how poor leadership leads to a business being mishandled from a shareholder perspective. Before declaring bankruptcy, the company had had about $100 million in annual revenues, though the part we acquired was just a portion of that. Its headquarters was a big castle outside Harrisburg with a lounge downstairs where people went and drank after work. It had an airplane and all kinds of cars, and there were other questionable activities going on at the company. Their IT department had budget of $8 million and 22 people. The business side was totally out of sync with excessive expenses that were not supported by revenues. We decided to buy only the six schools. I would say the odds of those schools surviving were about 20%; but the price was right and we were risk takers.

The schools had every problem that such institutions could possibly have. Faculty members were leaving. Student enrollments were dropping because no one knew how long the schools would remain open. Advertising, which could have helped recruit new students, had stopped. Accreditation agencies were about to withdraw their accreditation. For schools like these, which were two-year degree-granting colleges for computer programmers, nurses, health-care providers, and so on, this perfect storm of problems was almost the kiss of death.

Part of the reason several private schools got into this situation was that during the 1980s, a variety of people who had been in the S&L business and other lines of work unrelated to education got into this field. When they saw that they could get government funding for students whom they recruited for their schools, this tempted them to introduce highly questionable practices. Some of these were big, publicly held companies, but even they were misusing the system. Some of them would get people out of unemployment or soup kitchen lines and enroll them in schools, supposedly to help them reenter the workforce. These so-called students would often not show up to attend a single class, but the schools would get the tuition from the government. As soon as the

Department of Education realized what was going on, it came down with a hammer on such for-profit schools. And when they went belly up, no one wanted to buy these schools because their problems were so deep-rooted.

My colleague Gerard Francois, who had worked for Coopers & Lybrand and now is a principal of The Palmer Group, has been involved with analyzing career schools for a long time. He describes the schools that got into trouble this way: "Their senior executives had a lapse of judgment. In any company, in order to continue to succeed, you need to constantly improve your product, people, and marketing. Instead, these executives bought jets, and their shareholders paid the price because the company's surpluses were used for wrong purposes. They got greedy." Little wonder that most people saw such career schools as a terrible investment.

I had a different view. The more I looked at this business, the more I thought it was critical for the future of the American economy. If you look at how many people graduate from four-year colleges, that number is somewhat higher than 30%. The U.S. is the best in the world in relation to four-year institutions. But what about the other 60-plus percent? We are among the worst in the world. In the U.S., if you go on to college, that's your path to success. If you don't go on to college, no one seems to worry about you. In Philadelphia probably 50% of its working population is technically obsolete in today's world. The jobs they used to do have gone to Taiwan, Hong Kong, China, Mexico, or wherever. Those jobs just no longer exist here. People often ask, "Why can't we get jobs?"—but in my view, the question isn't so much why jobs aren't available, but why we aren't training people to do the jobs that *are* available.

It appeared to me that if we got into this business, it would fit my criterion of doing something meaningful and worthwhile—so we went ahead with the acquisition of the six schools, creating a company we named American Education Centers. When I met and spoke with the students, it helped me understand the impact our activities had. One time, I remember going to Atlanta to give the graduation speech at one of the schools. I met the president of the student government and asked her, "How did you come to be here?" She told me that after 15 to 20 years of marriage, her husband had left her. Before that, she had never held a job—but after her husband left, she had to provide for two children without having any professional skills. Initially she got a clerical job that paid $12,000 a year, and she took it despite knowing that she couldn't give her children the things they needed on that kind of salary. Meanwhile, she also enrolled at our school to become a legal stenographer. "And I will become one, after I graduate in three months," she said. I asked her how much she would make as a legal stenographer, and she replied, "If I were to go into Atlanta and take a job with a firm there, I would make more than $40,000. But I need to spend more time with my children, so I've already contracted with two local law firms—and I will make between $30,000 and $35,000 a year working for them." In other words, by learning the skills she needed at our school, she would double and possibly triple her compensation.

As I met more students, I realized that her story was typical. Our students would take advanced software courses and go out and start making $60,000. We trained nurses who would go out and earn $35,000 to $40,000. We had TV and radio technicians who went on to make $50,000. Our schools were able to take people who had a high-school degree and who might have been flipping burgers at McDonald's or Wendy's, and in two years, on a part-time basis, we could put them into a career where they could go out and double or triple their incomes. Two-thirds to three-quarters of the students were women. Almost all of them had children and full-time jobs. The majority were single parents. I looked at this situation and thought, "We are doing a great thing." We had hit a niche here about which I felt really good. As our operations developed, over time we came to acquire more schools. In all, we acquired 20 entities and never had one fail—which is unusual for an organization like ours.

At the time when we started buying schools, no one would lend us money because of all the questionable practices that were rife in this industry. We needed additional capital so I took on a partner who owned 45% of this business. My partner was Jim Walter, who had sold his home-building business, Jim Walter Corp., to the LBO experts Kohlberg Kravis Roberts in 1987 in a deal worth more than $3.3 billion. He had made a lot of money. Jim was an old-fashioned businessman, and he was the kind of person with whom I like to do business. When I went to see him—I knew him very well—I told him, "Jim, I am going into this business, and I would like you to be my partner." He said fine. I told him I did not know when we would be buying schools, but when we did, I would put in 55% and he would put in 45%; and apart from seller debt, we would not have to borrow any cash. He said that's fine. I asked what kind of arrangement we should come up with—and Jim said, "You just write it up, and it will be fine with me."

I sent Jim the shareholder agreement and called to ask if he had read it, and he said, "Absolutely not." His philosophy was to invest based on people...and he was a very smart investor. Jim made his investments based on people he knew, trusted, and respected. As a result, he did not have to worry about all the things that investors worry about today. He told me, "I know you're going to be fair. Nobody can put together a contract that is as good as two honest people working together."

This illustrates the importance of choosing the right people to do business with. I always bent over backward to resolve any ambiguities in Jim's favor, and he trusted me. That is why he was my partner until he passed away in January 2000. I bought back most of his interest that had been passed on to his children—except that he had told his wife that she should never sell her portion of this investment. He told her before he died that this was one investment to which she should hold on until we exited. She made a lot of money by taking Jim's advice. I learned a lot in this business about people. The faculty members at Wharton are good people. There may be a couple of bad apples, but by and large they are good folks. The same thing was true of the partners at Touche Ross—they also were good people. In the business world, you meet all sorts. The most important thing is to deal with people whom you can trust and who are honest. Therefore, if you ever plan to go into any kind of entrepreneurial venture, the most important thing to remember is that you must have two honest people doing business. The worst experiences I had in my 15-year career as an entrepreneur/investor occurred when I deviated from this rule and got involved with people who were not that way. Later I'll describe these painful experiences.

In addition to a financial partner, I needed an operational person who could run the business. After the first person we hired was not up to the job, I brought in a second person, and he was terrific in turning the schools around.

The person we hired to become the CEO of AEC was Bill Brooks. He had earlier run Spartan Aeronautics, a school that educated people who wanted to learn how to fly aircraft. He had dramatically improved the productivity of the business, which had gone from graduating 130 flight students to graduating 750 to 760 flight students, by doing simple but innovative things such as doing maintenance at midnight (so that the aircraft were not grounded for maintenance when the students needed to fly them). I was hoping that Brooks would be able to bring about a similar transformation at the career schools we were acquiring— and he succeeded in doing just that. Let me add a third point to the inviolate rules of adequate due diligence and doing business with people you respect and trust. Take whatever time is necessary and, within reason, spend whatever is required to get the right CEO—it's hard (if not impossible) to succeed without having the right person leading the ship.

Our experience in turning the schools around taught us a great deal about leadership in an entrepreneurial context. What did we have to do? Everything. We had to hire almost all new administrative people. Some of the faculty remained, but we had to replace a substantial number. We put in new systems. We put in an online system that told us everything about our business—how many people applied for the courses; where that application was in the process; where we got those applicants; all our financial data, our bad debts data, and everything we needed to know. All this was available to us online and in real time. It was probably the most sophisticated management information system that any private group in our industry had.

In addition, we had to physically change essentially every facility. For example, in Cincinnati, Ohio, the school was in an old electric company building that was falling down. We had to move to a new building in a different part of town. We had to reestablish relations with all the regulators and put in new procedures. We had to get rid of many of the admissions people because they were using questionable practices and that is one of the things that got the schools into trouble. We put in new computer laboratories that were so state-of-the-art even larger institutions could not match them. They seemed like space-age facilities. We had to change everything from top to bottom—and we did it as though we were going to own these companies forever.

Initially when we started acquiring the schools in 1993, they were cheap because we bought them out of bankruptcy. As we went through the 1990s, however, the proprietary school industry came back in vogue and we were competing against everybody else. After the first purchases, we did not buy any more out of bankruptcy. There are only 3,000 proprietary schools in the U.S. We had a list of all of them. We sent them letters, we went and visited them, and when we found a school that looked like it would fit with our portfolio, we bought it. As prices went up, we started working with T L Ventures, a venture fund headed by Bob Keith. They provided funds for a minority position in some of our investments and gave us full operating control. They have been great partners.

We kept some key issues in mind while targeting schools for acquisition. We wanted schools that were compatible with the kind of training we did. Geographically we focused on the Midwest.

Someone once asked me, "Why do you like this region so much?" I said, "Because I understand those people." The Midwest was a good region for us to concentrate on because it had a lot of people who needed the kind of retraining we offered. They generally had favorable state rules for proprietary schools. Typically, we would look for a mom-and-pop operation, where they were getting ready to retire or just getting tired of the school business, because it is a difficult business. It is as bad as the restaurant business, because you have to be there all the time. You have to make your admissions work. There are lots of federal regulations. We looked for somebody who wanted to sell out in a good location. Typically they would not be doing well, though they would not necessarily be losing money.

We would take that situation and triple the enrollments. We could go into a school that had been operating for 20 years and through installing new leadership and modern techniques—advertising, admissions, and other systems—we could dramatically build up their enrollments. One school that we bought, in Fort Wayne, Indiana, had 77 students when we bought it and we were able to increase the number to 750 in a relatively short period. We had the ability to do that—giving people a very good education and a very high placement rate when they left. So we kept buying schools. That is how we built the business.

We tripled enrollments also by doing innovative things. Let me give two examples. First, most proprietary schools start, just as most colleges do, two or three times a year. If a student decides to go to school, he or she might have to wait three or four months to start. Well, students who want to go to a professional school don't want to wait that long. Once they have decided to go to school, they want to get going. So we started sessions 12 times a year. To my knowledge, no one else was doing that at the time. The faculty members didn't like it very well because it disrupted their class schedules. And we had to configure the curriculum in a way that allowed for a very different way of doing things. But it accommodated the students who wanted to get started right away.

Second, we introduced what we called a 50-50 program. If you are a working mother or a single parent with children at home, your biggest problem in going to school will be finding the time to go there two or three times a week. To deal with this issue, we split each course into two parts: what you would do in the classroom and what you would do online. We gave each student a computer so that they could log on from their work or from the office. By doing that, we cut in half the time the students had to be in our facility. This approach gave them a lot more flexibility, but it still gave them a classroom experience, which they needed. We couldn't teach these courses exclusively online.

Meanwhile, what the 50-50 approach did for us internally was to double our capacity. If you can have twice as many students as you used to have because they are only in a classroom one-half as much of the time, then that is a big thing. It went a long way in helping us reach double or triple the enrollments at each school.

The financial performance of the schools improved dramatically. As Brooks, our CEO, recalls, when he came to work for us, "we were on track to lose $700,000. We made a complete change, and we ended up losing $300,000. The next year we made $250,000."

One other important change we made was to meet the demands of the job market. Traditionally, what many proprietary schools have done is to focus on just one area of instructions, such as computer software or travel. The problem with that approach is that if the technology sector goes through a bust (which it did) or the bottom falls out of the travel agency business (which did happen), it drags the schools down as well. We decided to look at what the market was asking for, and to focus on those courses. As a result, while a lot of schools still had travel courses at a time when the airlines were slashing payments to travel agents and travel agencies were going out of business, we got rid of all our travel courses. We got rid of all the court reporter transcription courses. We were one of the highest in the U.S. in terms of people passing that test, 14%. The national average was 9%. Would you want to be training people in an area where only 14% of the people got jobs? We got out of that. We asked, "What does the market want?" If the market wanted health-care people, we should shift right into the new area. We might not cut down on other areas completely, but we would change our emphasis.

Gerard Francois, my partner, says that our ability to offer different kinds of programs protected us against the risk of demand for certain types of courses drying up unexpectedly. "We had three key programs: IT, business, and health," he says. "When the IT bubble burst in the spring of 2001, demand for those courses declined but demand for health-care courses went up." These strategies allowed us to keep growing.

Exit Strategy

We did this for a decade. As word spread about our activities, a lot of people tried to buy us out. We were probably as good a privately held proprietary schools group as there was in the U.S. While we were not the biggest, we were certainly among the biggest—our annual revenues had grown to around $50 million to $60 million. When people asked if we were interested in selling, we said no.

Eventually some folks from Education Management Corp., which I consider the country's best publicly held proprietary school group, approached us. The founder, Bob Knutson, and its CEO, Jock McKernan, the former governor of Maine, came to our office. Their approach to us was simple: They said, "We know you don't want to sell, but some day you will want to exit from your investment. What would it take for you to consider selling now?" We had essentially no debt, and we had paid back all the investment we had put in plus some. I said that for us to consider a sale, it would have to be an offer of more than $100 million in cash, and you would have to hire every one of our people. They said, "Okay, we'll do it." Ultimately we sold the school business for essentially $120 million in cash. That was a big win. EDMC lived up to every one of the things they told us they would do, including hiring all of our people. Bill Brooks, our CEO, eventually became the chief operating officer for all of Education Management.

After the sale of our proprietary schools business to EDMC, we acquired another education business in San Francisco, called Fire Solutions. This company, which was established in 1998, provides online training to brokers and others who have to be licensed or have to take exams to move up in the world in insurance, brokerage, and other industries.

Our most recent acquisition in The Palmer Group tested our resolve to exercise great care in selecting each new purchase. It is Salem International University, a university in Salem, West Virginia. It has about 700 students on campus and a few hundred online. It is a school that has a rich background, with several well-known people going there including a prominent senator and a former governor. As with many primarily liberal arts colleges, it started to fall on hard times more than 10 years ago. Some foreign investors came in and, in effect, controlled this non-profit school by buying the land and buildings and putting some of their representatives on the board of trustees. A Japanese group owned the school for several years and then sold it to another group in Singapore. Between the two groups, they invested upward of $30 million over the 10-year period.

When we looked at this situation, it was bleeding cash to the tune of about $500,000 to $600,000 a month and was within a few weeks of bankruptcy. This was the most difficult acquisition we ever made. We had very little time to look at the situation since they were going to be forced into bankruptcy in the very near future. They needed cash immediately and they had every problem you can imagine. They had problems with the accrediting agencies, problems with the federal and state governments, problems with their creditors, and on and on and on.

The school, however, presented a group of very attractive opportunities. We are now in an era when more and more education is going to be provided online. Salem International University had accreditation with the regional accrediting body, which is the highest accreditation you can get; it had an online system; and it had graduate programs including a masters in business administration and a masters in education. This is a very powerful foundation in today's education world. In addition, we were fairly confident that the Department of Education was going to drop the requirement of having 50% in class attendance in online programs, which they did later, and this would make the situation here even more valuable.

We did as much due diligence as we could in the time we had. We saw that this was a high-risk, high-reward situation and decided to involve a venture capital fund that would lower our risk. We put in capital before we closed, getting the land and buildings as collateral. We then continued our due diligence while having to put in additional capital and concluded the deal essentially within 60 days. There were other potential buyers involved but they just couldn't move that fast. When we got through with our due diligence, we went to the foreign ownership and gave them an extremely lengthy list of everything we found and told them that we would give them only $500,000 for the land and buildings and they would have to forgive about $7 million in debt from the university. It seemed like a relatively low price to pay for 28 buildings, 500 acres, and an operating school to boot. We got an estimate on the replacement cost on the buildings and that alone was $78 million. But these buildings were worth nothing if you didn't have a functioning school, and the $500,000 was just the tip of the iceberg relative to the money we were going to have to put in. We immediately had to infuse $5 million to keep the operation going.

We then went about what we had learned to do fairly well. We got a CEO who had been through school turnarounds on several occasions and asked if he would take this on for a two-year period until we got our permanent CEO. We turned the not-for-profit school into a for-profit entity, and that required us to apply through the state. West Virginia is a very good place to do business and it went smoothly. We talked to the Department of Education, other federal agencies, the accrediting agencies, the creditors, the state education agency, and many others and were able to buy some time.

Then we went about cutting costs. We cut out some non-essential employees, although this had already been done to a considerable degree and we didn't have much room here. We dropped all the watersport programs, and we got rid of an equestrian program that was costing a couple of hundred thousand dollars a year and put the equestrian center itself up for sale. We donated some land and historic buildings to a local foundation and took a big tax deduction. We brought in some new faculty and all new key officers working for the CEO. In 24 months we were approaching a break-even point. The previous owners had put $30 million into this operation and all they had to show for it financially was that it was continuing to drain $500,000 to $600,000 a month in cash.

We are now on our way to building our online operation. We hope to have 6,000 to 10,000 students in these programs within five years, and we will have a very valuable enterprise. We are going to operate this school as though we are going to own it forever. We are going to upgrade the quality throughout the institution and we are going to be very proud of what we do. In the process we are going to do good things for a lot of students and West Virginia. We are the biggest employer in Salem, and we are going to be good community citizens and help provide economic impact to this very depressed region. And we are going to feel good about what we do and have a lot of fun along the way.

This is how it goes in entrepreneurial leadership if you know what you are doing. By the time we got to buying professional schools, we had learned some very hard lessons from ventures that didn't go all that well—at least in the beginning. In effect, we learned about the pitfalls firsthand.

When Entrepreneurial Leadership Fails: Errors and Potential Pitfalls

Probably the most dangerous pitfall confronting a would-be entrepreneur is inexperience. Whether the potential entrepreneur has an idea for a service or product to commercialize, or feels the urge to become an entrepreneur without a specific plan for how to proceed, there is a good chance that he or she lacks experience in pioneering new ventures. This was certainly the case with me and my partners when we began the Palmer Group. Our mistakes were a textbook lesson in what to avoid.

The first company we bought was Spike's Trophies in Philadelphia. It was the city's oldest trophy, plaque, and business-gift manufacturer, with sales of a couple of million dollars. This investment was a negative learning experience—in part because we failed to do proper due diligence. I overpaid for the company because it turned out that our due diligence wasn't effective enough to spot some adjustments that should have been made to the financial statements. I had borrowed money from Mellon Bank to buy the company, and when these facts emerged we almost immediately went into default.

That was when I had my first real personal experience with bankers. Mellon Bank was going through a difficult period and was trying to clean up its loan portfolio. I told the bankers, "What are you worried about? I am going to pay you." They said, in that case, please put your personal signature on this loan (I was not personally liable). I said, "I don't want to put my personal signature on the loan, because you have my word. You are going to get paid." Mellon Bank said it would rather have us pay 60% right away to close out the loan rather than the whole amount later. Reluctantly, I agreed—even though I did not want to do it that way. Eventually the problems were resolved and we kept the company for 12 or 13 years before selling it to the employees. They were overjoyed.

The experience with Spike's Trophies taught me that I didn't know enough about buying companies, and that I had to be more careful next time. Although I had been entrepreneurial at Wharton and also at Touche Ross, I had not been an entrepreneur in the buying business sense. But the school of hard knocks had more lessons in store for me.

We then went into the payroll business. I went to a friend who had been successful in that business and told him I wanted to go into the same business. He said, "I know two great people who used to work for me, and they could help you out." At that point I made a basic mistake: I didn't check them out with anyone else. I thought that if these people had been working for him for 10 years, they must be good. I should have known better.

We carefully drew up a contract that described the way we would be involved and defined their role as the day-to-day operators. It soon became clear to me, though, that in their mind, we were only one thing—a source of capital. We owned 85% of the company, and they wanted more capital as we went along. Their argument was that the more capital that was available to get new accounts, the bigger the payroll business would be. They were not willing to listen to our views about the way the business should be run, especially about controlling expenses and growing profits. They just wanted to keep getting money from us so that they could build the operation faster and faster. Eventually we faced an impasse. The president kept telling me that he was going to quit because we did not do the things he wanted us to do, and when my patience was exhausted, I said, "Fine, you just did." He couldn't believe I said that. I did not have to fire him—he threatened to quit, and I accepted.

Then I went through a dismal period where they tried to force me to sell out to them. They sued, arguing that I was trying to force them out, and it went to arbitration. This was a little company with a couple of million dollars in sales, and the fees from arbitration were several hundred thousand dollars. It was a nightmare that went on and on for more than a year. Eventually we sold the company.

These painful experiences happened because I went into business with people I shouldn't have. The lesson is that we didn't do enough homework on the people we were dealing with. We should have looked more closely to understand what their motivations were for entering into this deal with us. This would have helped us to determine what their goals were, what they had done previously in other difficult situations, and they interacted with their customers, vendor, and other partners in the past. In other words, we needed to be sure their goals would be aligned with ours.

These and several other experiences were the pitfalls I encountered. I took away from them three lessons on how to avoid them. The first is that as a part of any due diligence that you do, be sure that you check the references of anyone with whom you are going to do business. Check with not just the people they give as references but also the others whom you find yourself who might be able to give you an unbiased opinion. That is much more important than how glib someone sounds in an interview.

The second lesson, if you are buying an existing business that you intend to run, is to make certain that the financial figures you are furnished are accurate and factual.

The third lesson concerns the arrangements you may have with partners in the venture. If you set up a partnership—even with people you believe to be very honorable—you are inviting trouble if you set it up as a 50-50 venture, or one in which the management thinks you are a silent partner, or one in which they control the management of customer relations in the enterprise even if you own 85% of the stock. Somebody needs to be the leader and have a shareholder's agreement that clearly states where the control vests. If you have a partner, you may not always see eye-to-eye on every issue, and sooner or later, someone will need to make a decision. If there are two equal partners, sooner or later you generally have problems. The payroll company was probably the worst experience I had in 15 years as an entrepreneur. It was my own fault and I take responsibility for it.

There are other pitfalls that we did not encounter, but that other entrepreneurs have encountered, that need to be mentioned. Tom Presby, whom I have known since our days together at Touche Ross, works closely with CEOs of entrepreneurial companies. This has made him a shrewd observer of errors that entrepreneurial leaders make. According to him, "The first mistake entrepreneurs make is not making money. They should understand that loss forecasts are always achieved and often exceeded. The biggest failure I see among entrepreneurial leaders is that they are willing to defer achieving profitability. There is no such thing as an excellent organization that is unprofitable."

Another common error, he says, is not raising enough money. "I meet with entrepreneurs all the time, and they don't know what they need," he says. "They are too focused on one aspect of their operation to the exclusion of others, and then other things wither. To succeed as an entrepreneurial leader, you need breadth of thought. You have to be a people person to build an organization that focuses on every important activity, not just the one the CEO thinks is most important."

This leads me to my final point about entrepreneurs: If they are successful, they will find themselves leading in a different context.

Leading in Another Context

Successful entrepreneurs find that as the business grows, so does the organization. What worked for them in the early days will probably not work when they are responsible for a growing and increasingly complex business. Tom Presby, who just told us about certain pitfalls, points out that the best entrepreneurial leaders recognize that they need to evolve. "I know CEOs who started out not being too involved in finance, but now because of Sarbanes-Oxley are involved in finance at tremendous levels of detail," Presby says. "At another company, the CEO is very entrepreneurial but not systematic enough. All this shows that leadership is not a static activity. Leaders have to change and develop new skills and interests. They might have to do things they find repugnant so that they can keep building their organizations and themselves."

Leadership and Social Entrepreneurship

Bill Gates caused a stir in the summer of 2006 when he announced he would gradually give up his responsibilities at Microsoft to work much more actively with the Bill and Melinda Gates Foundation. This foundation focuses on global poverty and hunger, global health, and education, especially inequalities in the U.S. educational system The significance of that pronouncement increased further when Warren Buffett, who knows Gates well, said he would donate $31 billion in the form of 10 million shares of Berkshire Hathaway stock to the Gates Foundation, bringing its assets to more than $60 billion.

In recent years, entrepreneurs from George Soros to Nobel Laureate Mohammed Yunus have chosen to focus on social problems—although they may lack the resources of Gates or Buffett. As a result, entrepreneurial leadership in the nonprofit sector has become vitally important—and before ending this chapter, I would like to address this unique context and the special challenges such leaders face.

These leaders' goal is often to prove to themselves as well as their constituents that in addition to building a profitable company, they can also make a difference to society. In a few cases, the not-for-profit enterprise takes on a momentum of its own and makes as dramatic a contribution to society as the leader's for-profit activities. For this process to work, the leader must be able to translate his or her business leadership skills effectively to the nonprofit world.

John DiIulio, an expert in Jesuit leadership and a highly respected professor at the University of Pennsylvania, says he often talks to business leaders who want to become philanthropists. "I tell them not to leave their skills in the corporate office," he says. "The principles of leadership are the same, though the context is different."

Bill Gates is a good example of a leader who has applied his business acumen to the nonprofit context. "Gates found people who knew what he wanted to achieve—and focused on achieving measurable outcomes," DiIulio says. Another instance is that of William E. Simon, the former secretary of the U.S. Treasury during the Nixon administration. With his son Bill, Simon played a role in the development of PAX TV network, says DiIulio. "They asked if there was a market for a television network that aired programs with no sex and violence," he says. "They conducted surveys and approached it as any social scientist would. They approached it analytically—and they found that there were people who strongly believed in the value of wholesome television. They did not lose their sense of analyzing market demand before plunging in."

According to DiIulio, an important difference between leadership in the corporate and nonprofit worlds is that "in the nonprofit world, there is no bottom line. You have to have measurable impact, but in the nonprofit world, just as in government, how things get done is as important as what gets accomplished. This emphasis on process is very important." Leaders from the corporate world need to understand that difference in context.

One of the most important changes in nonprofit organizations in recent years has been the infusion of corporate leadership principles, DiIulio notes. "The attention to measurable results and high-yield philanthropy has been the result of corporate principles being applied in the nonprofit context," he says. "In the nonprofit world, the focus is on getting the boulder to the top of the hill. When people look for advice on leadership, they look to corporate leaders. You may be operating in the context of a nonprofit, but in the end, you need the discipline of being able to say whether you've got the boulder up the hill or not. You may take the context into account, but you've also got to take the boulder up the hill."

Virginia Clark, who worked for the University of Pennsylvania before moving to Washington, D.C., as head of fundraising for the Smithsonian Institution, explains that the world of nonprofits is similar as well as dissimilar to academia. She says, "In academia, you have faculty who do research, some who teach, others who provide services to students—and an infrastructure of staff to support them. At the Smithsonian, we have some researchers, others who deal with the public, and an infrastructure to support them. In some ways, this makes them similar."

At the same time, Clark says, "there also are ways in which academic institutions and nonprofits like the Smithsonian are not similar. In academia, a certain number of students come in every year, they pay tuition, and then they graduate and become alumni. That gives some predictability to the institution's cash flow. At the Smithsonian and other nonprofit institutions, the public comes in all the time. Nonprofits don't have the predictable cash flow that you have in academia. Some museums depend on blockbuster exhibits to raise revenues, but they are far more vulnerable to factors like the weather than academic institutions."

These similarities and differences have major implications for leadership. "Because cash flow is so unpredictable, you have to be rigorous in long-range planning for the future in nonprofit organizations," says Clark. "In academia, you can get caught up in short-term thinking, but in a nonprofit you have to be disciplined and keep your long-term goals in mind." Another implication, according to Clark, is that nonprofit organizations need leaders with greater strength of character and personality than might be essential in academia. "The reason is that you don't have a strong safety net or infrastructure around you in a nonprofit," Clark says.

Leadership at the Smithsonian has its own challenges. "The Congress gives us a fair amount of money but we don't belong in anyone's constituency," Clark explains. "If we were in Chicago, for example, we could marshal the resources of the Congress representatives from Illinois, but we are in Washington, D.C., and the mall, so we are everybody's. To deal with this situation, we have to make our case correctly so that we can argue things from a purely financial view. We have to be able to make a nonemotional, financial case for our needs."

Clark says that she also ensures that "our board of directors and best donors know that case, so that they can bring it up with the Senators and Congress representatives in their constituencies. We have to position ourselves as 'America's museums' and make it an emotional appeal."

In sum, Clark notes that leading in the context of nonprofits has unique challenges: "Leadership in dealing with the uncertainty involves making a strong financial case, aligning our constituents behind the case, and also an emotional appeal. Other nonprofits would have to follow a similar process. Whether you are an art museum in Chattanooga, Tennessee, or the Smithsonian, you would need to follow these same steps. It's applicable to most nonprofits."

Summary

- If you are acquiring a business, do your homework—your due diligence. You are never going to know as much as you should know, but you need to know as much as you can in the period you have until you make your decision.

- Deal with the right partners. If you deal with good people, your chances are infinitely better of having a happy, productive, rewarding outcome in the end. If you deal with the wrong people, the odds are heavily stacked against you and in any case it is going to be a miserable journey.

- If you are not going to operate the endeavor yourself, spend the time necessary to find a top CEO. After the decision of buying an enterprise or not, this is the most important decision you are going to make. I view myself as a good judge of people, but I am right only about half the time. This doesn't mean that half the time when I am wrong the people I've hired have turned out to be disasters; they have just not been as good as they needed to be for the position. Some people who make an incredible impression are really only about an inch deep.

- Once you have made a tentative decision about who to hire, you need to do in-depth reference checks. It should be exhaustive, and not just with the people whom you are given as references. You know what they are going to say.

- If you have found the CEO and the leadership team, let them do their job. If the CEO can't run the business by your standards, you have to get a new CEO. Good CEOs don't want to be in an environment where they get their orders over the phone from some investor every morning.

- Don't forget that you are the owner so you better stay close to what is going on. This requires very effective communication and an ability to know about problems very fast.

- Don't go into 50-50 partnerships even with good people. One person has to be in control.

- At some point you have to decide whether you are going to go ahead with a particular venture. You can only study it so much. I know of one venture capitalist who never made a deal. He just kept kicking the tires until he found something that bothered him, and then he walked away. Maybe you can't really call him a venture capitalist.

- Risk is tied to potential return. That's what they teach you at Wharton and it's true. I know of very few deals that have terrific potential returns with no risk attached, so in most cases you are going to take on the amount of risk that is commensurate with the potential return. So consider that carefully into your decision. On the other hand, I doubt if you want your portfolio to be one very high-risk singular situation that has tremendous potential but puts all your eggs in one basket. You may need several ventures to spread the risk.

- Treat your investments as if you were going to own them forever. You should run them as if they were a company in which you have pride and want to promote excellence in what it does, and reflect your character and the way you do business.

- The business sooner or later has to come down to profits, so make it sooner.

- Develop your leadership skills as your business grows and becomes more complex.

- Some operators think that investors are just an endless source of capital. That is not a healthy mindset. They should be turning a profit as early as possible. Profits should be used to fund new ventures and products, and if more investment is needed, this should be done very deliberately. Investors need to buy in on the need for infusing more capital. Capital infusion to cover operating losses over an extended period is bad.

- Communicate your thoughts clearly. In academia or nonprofit environments you may often use subtlety and diplomacy in your approach. Here you need to be straightforward and very clear relative to your position. If you don't, it can cost you money or a deal.

Chapter 8

THE ACADEMIC ORGANIZATION: LEARNING FROM THE WHARTON EXPERIENCE

Leadership in colleges and universities is a very complex exercise. The number of constituents multiplies enormously over what I experienced when I headed Touche Ross. In trying to do something for one group, I found that others probably felt that their ox was being gored. The constituents with whom a leader in academia—whether a dean, provost, or president—must contend include the university administration, faculty, alumni, students, staff, accrediting bodies, and so on. I later came to feel that if I got up in the morning and asked for a vote on whether the sun should come up tomorrow, after considerable debate the vote would be 51–49 and I could not be sure in advance whether it would be for or against.

In this chapter I again step forward, as I did in previous chapters, and describe my experience in a different context, as dean of a major business school. The reason why I think my experiences will help readers is that they help to illustrate how leadership can operate and also potentially succeed in collegial environments. In the following pages, I describe how I came to be appointed to the job and how there was initial skepticism among the faculty that an "accountant" without a graduate degree could lead a business school with a distinguished faculty. My first meeting with the full faculty nearly derailed my deanship until I found a way to connect with them. In this chapter, I describe a number of initiatives that I undertook at Wharton that required the cooperation of the faculty and administration. I explain how my experience taught me about the pitfall that so many leaders in business ignore and therefore fail at effective leadership in the academic context. I describe how success in academic leadership can be a sound background when leading in other contexts that academic leaders may encounter as a part of their jobs. Finally, I give the last words to three faculty members at Wharton who summarize the style that academic leaders need to adopt in order to succeed.

Though the academic world is unusual in many ways, it shares some characteristics with other contexts that can make this chapter useful even if you are not leading in academia.

Context: The Academic Organization

It was the 17th of March 1983. I was in Montreal, attending a meeting of the international leadership of Touche Ross, when my assistant came to me and said, "You had better take a break. We have a problem."

The problem, as she explained it, was that the *Washington Post* had run a story in that morning's edition that said I was about to be named the next dean of the Wharton School, and none of the people in the meeting or in our firm knew about it. So at the end of that day I told my colleagues about the *Washington Post* story. I explained that I had spoken to the university and had expressed interest in the position—but no one had formally offered me a job, nor had I accepted it. "I just want you all to be aware of that," I said.

The fact that I had been speaking to Wharton about becoming the dean would not have surprised people who knew me well. As I said in Chapter 4, "The Organization of Peers: Leading Your Equals," the nominating committee at Touche Ross had approached me about extending my term past 10 years—or at least to submit a proposal to that effect to the partnership—but I had decided against doing that. Ten years is a long time to be in that job—or probably in any job.

After much thought about what to do next, I tentatively decided that being connected with a business school, possibly as the dean, might be an interesting and challenging new career. Soon after I had made that tentative decision, I got a call from Bill Ruder, founder of Ruder and Finn, the New York–based communications agency. I had worked closely with Ruder on PR issues, and I had told him about my interest in the academic world. He said, "Wharton is looking for a dean; would you like to go down and talk with them?" My first reaction was that the timing did not seem right, but he asked, "Russ, do you think the world is going to adhere to your timing? You have an incredible opportunity here, and it's generally what you want to do. Are you going to go and visit Wharton or not?" He had a point, so I decided to visit the school.

When I went to Wharton, I learned more about the situation. The University of Pennsylvania had been searching for a dean for more than a year, and it had taken longer than anyone could have imagined. The Search Committee had gone through more than 100 names and interviewed lots of people, some of whom would not commit to the job full-time. When I met with the search committee, I told them that I could assure them of one thing: "I am not coming here so I can write a book, or run for office, or use this as a steppingstone to my next job. I am coming here, if you want me, with just one thing in mind—how to make Wharton the number-one business school." This was the first time I articulated my vision for the school, but it was by no means the last. Whatever else I said, I think that statement struck a responsive chord.

When I met with the Search Committee a second time, they asked me, among other things, how I would feel about going into the Provost's staff conference.

"Pardon me, but first you'll have to tell me what that is," I said. "That's where the deans get together and go over the professors' appointments and promotions," was the explanation.

The question seemed to refer to my lack of a Ph.D. that would be expected of a dean at Wharton. I said, "I think the question you are asking me is, how could someone with a nonacademic background, who doesn't have in-depth knowledge of refereed journals and academic accomplishment and who doesn't have an advanced degree, be prepared to discuss such matters? It seems to me what you really want to know is if I am going to feel intimidated going into that academic setting with all those other people who have their 'union cards,' i.e., Ph.D. degrees."

"Yes, that's essentially what we are asking you," the interviewers said.

I believed that my experience leading Touche Ross would actually serve me well and I answered, "I work in a firm with 20,000 professionals. I have had at least 10 Ph.D.'s work with me, and I have never had any problem with them. I hope that answers your question. I know I'm going to have to do a lot more homework for the Provost's staff conference than the other members do, but I'm prepared to do that."

In fairly short order the search committee concluded that I should be the 10th dean of the Wharton School in the spring of 1983—and the first to be appointed from outside of academia.

A challenge just as difficult as convincing the search committee now lay before me: convincing the faculty that someone with only a bachelor's degree from Michigan State University was qualified to lead them. As I had told the Search Committee, I thought that my job was to lead the school in attaining our collective vision and that I did not need to know in depth all about the latest finance research. What I did need, among other things, was the ability to recruit top-caliber faculty to build the best departments to attract the best students and help them get top jobs. I believed my job was to build superb academic departments for Wharton by bringing in and helping promote and nurturing the top people in the various fields, and conveying their knowledge effectively to students in the classroom. If I could do that, it didn't matter how much or how little I knew about the details of research. I did not see my lack of an academic background as a problem. The question was how to get this view across to the faculty.

My first meeting with the full faculty began badly. A meeting had been set up at which Sheldon Hackney, the university president, and Tom Ehrlich, the provost, were to be in attendance. The faculty members—who numbered well over 100—came to a small amphitheater at the bottom of Steinberg Hall–Dietrich Hall, the building where the Dean's office is located. This was my first real test—and everyone knew it, including me.

I got up to speak. I had thought quite a bit about what I should say. The gist of my message to the professors was this: If you expect me to give you my vision for Wharton as a business school today, I am not going to do that; I believe my job is to lead the school in attaining our collective vision. I had expected there would be a very good response to that point, but as I scanned the crowd, there was no response at all, just silence. From the corner of my eye, I could see some people reading papers.

With growing apprehension, I continued with the other remarks I had prepared. I had decided to speak for just 15 to 20 minutes. In my previous career I had addressed a lot of meetings, and I can tell whether I have people's attention or whether they generally agree with what I am saying. I knew I was getting nowhere with this group. I could imagine what they were thinking—that the Search Committee had gone mad. Most professors in the room probably believed that the Search Committee had horsed around for over a year, and when they couldn't find anyone they could agree on, they pulled in an accountant with only an undergraduate degree from a state university who had never been in academia. Clearly, everyone on the Search Committee had to be crazy. Wharton had never had a dean who did not have a Ph.D. and had not had some previous connection to the school.

I decided to take a risk. First impressions are crucial. I knew if I didn't make the correct impression, it might take months to overcome that handicap, and I didn't have much of the 15 minutes left. So I said, "I do know one thing. My reason for being here is to help Wharton become the number-one business school. I have done a little research on this, and I think I know where we stand now. If we are going to be the number-one school, we must have the best faculty. If we are to have the best faculty, we will have to pay commensurate with our competition, which I believe is Harvard and Stanford. Right now, I believe that you all on average make only two-thirds of what professors at Harvard and Stanford make, and I'm going to do my best to change that."

Sheldon Hackney, the president, seemed to turn white. He could hardly believe what he had just heard. Tom Ehrlich, the provost, had a restrained smile on his face. The mood in the room suddenly changed. The faculty members sat up and started paying attention. Those who were reading papers put them down. I could almost hear them thinking, "Maybe this guy isn't all bad after all. Maybe we should give him a chance and see what he can do."

This echoed one of the leadership principles I described in the first chapter. To be a leader you must understand the self-interest of your constituents. Probably every faculty member in that meeting wanted and felt they deserved more compensation— every single one of them. They might have had a plethora of views on every other matter, but this was the one thing they could all agree on. I had researched the compensation issue carefully; I knew that at that time, senior faculty members at Harvard and Stanford made considerably more than the average salary of a senior Wharton faculty member. They had started out by seeing me as someone who had no academic credentials; now they saw me as someone who had the courage to stand up in front of the president and provost in his first faculty meeting and say, "I'm going to do my best to make this happen because you deserve it." What I didn't tell them was that only half of them deserved it and probably deserved more, and the other half proba- bly didn't. I didn't get much feedback after this speech—but I did hear that it was "positively received."

First the Faculty

To make the collective vision a reality, we developed a program called the Plan for Pre-eminence. Its goal was to make Wharton the top business school in the U.S., and it had many different elements. For the plan to succeed, we needed every constituency at the school—faculty, staff, students, alumni, and so forth—to pull together to achieve it. Early on I realized that it would help if I were able to win over the senior faculty, so we created the Faculty Advisory Board made up of important opinion makers in the faculty. They not only offered good advice but gave me credibility with the rest of the faculty because it became known that I was in frequent consultation with the board on key decisions.

After I was appointed dean, but before I officially took office, I had gone down once a week while Don Carroll, who preceded me as dean, was still there, and talked to whoever wanted to meet with me. In addition, I sought out meetings with members of the faculty whom I particularly wanted to get to know. Interestingly, but not unexpectedly, many of the people who wanted to see me wanted something. They didn't like their compensation; they wanted a promotion; or they wanted to head something or keep something as it was.

Before embarking on the Plan for Pre-eminence, I talked for more than 200 hours with various people at the school—heads of departments, key faculty members, students, and key administrators. The questions I had asked them included, "What do we do here? How do we do it? What are the problems in getting to where we want to go? How much money is it going to take?"

I also asked the administrative leadership team, "Who is our customer?" They looked at me as if I were someone from outer space who didn't understand that in academia you have no customers. The fact is, the attitude of some people in academia is that academic institutions would be wonderful places if they did not have to put up with students. After a few discussions, we determined that Wharton did, perhaps, have customers—and that they were the students who paid high fees to come to the school and the companies that recruited them. After we got to that point, it became clear that we ought to concentrate more on the experience that students had while they were at the school. We also focused on and improved our treatment of companies that came to campus to hire them.

After listening to their ideas for at least 200 hours, I came up with a tentative plan and then decided to form a strategic planning group. We picked out key faculty members and one or two people from outside, including John Harris, a consultant from Booz Allen Hamilton, to serve as the facilitator. We went away and spent two or three days with this group and retooled the plan and came back and presented it to a group of the top faculty opinion makers. Then we got consensus among various other groups until finally we went to the faculty and presented the plan for preeminence. By the time we went to the faculty meeting, a great majority of the key faculty had been involved with and signed on to the plan.

The plan focused attention on several major initiatives that I believed were crucial to achieve the goal of making Wharton the top business school. One key element was that we would recruit top faculty members for the school. Other crucial elements included fundraising, student recruitment, revising the curriculum, revamping Executive Education, improving the physical facilities, upgrading technology, and so on. During my tenure at the school, we brought in 111 new faculty members. With help from our faculty, I identified the top faculty in the various disciplines, and then I visited Chicago, Yale, Harvard, and other universities to see whether I could bring them to Wharton. I saw that as a big part of my job.

My approach to the faculty from other institutions varied. Sometimes, we would bring them to Wharton to give a lecture. Then I would tell the person, "I know you are very happy where you are, but let's just fantasize for a moment. What would it take to get you to move from there to Wharton?" And they would tell me.

Some of the faculty members did not want to teach as much as they were doing; one person from Yale wanted to expand the program he had been running there; many wanted more research funds. Once I knew what they wanted, I would say, "Okay, I'll do it." Sometimes, despite this approach, the people I was trying to recruit did not come to Wharton, but they thought about it seriously and they liked our way of thinking about how to attract people. And many of them did end up coming to Wharton. Soon some of the top professors in the U.S. were moving to Wharton. Among them were Sandy Grossman in finance; Ian MacMillan, a management professor who came to the school from New York University; David Larcker, a professor of accounting who was recruited from Northwestern University; and Robert Litzenberger, from Stanford.

Another important recruiting method was called the "term professorship"—it was the first time I know that anybody had used it, though now it has become quite common. We would go to the best of the young academics coming out of Ph.D. programs and we would offer them five-year term "professorships" with research budgets of $50,000. They could use $10,000 a year for five years and spend it on their research. We would tell the professors that with these resources for research, they would have a better shot at promotion—and they could call themselves the XYZ Term Professor in Finance. Again, some of the university bureaucrats went wild. They asked, "How could you introduce these term professorships and call new faculty members 'term professors'?" But nevertheless we started hiring the best young professors. Sure, other schools could offer them money, but no one could offer them a term professorship that they could place behind their name and $50,000 they could use for research spread over five years. We got Pat Harker, who later became Wharton's dean before going on to become President of the University of Delaware, under one of these term professorships.

That is how we built Wharton's faculty. It was critical to have the finest faculty to make Wharton the number-one business school, because the faculty are at the core of everything the school does. What does Wharton do? It teaches, does research, and disseminates knowledge. Wharton teaches—and if that is true, I felt we would need top-caliber faculty who not only did great research but also were outstanding teachers. Wharton's mission is to disseminate knowledge to students and others. That requires faculty. That is the core of the school's purpose.

I saw the role of the faculty at Wharton like that of the partners at Touche Ross. We either had the best partners or the worst ones. If we had the best partners, we would be the best firm. It was as simple and as difficult as that. Sometimes MBAs and many businesspeople think the most important things are formulas, algorithms, getting an edge, and so on. People are most important, and we should spend a lot of our time attracting them, developing them, training them, and leading them.

Rationalizing the Curriculum

In addition to recruiting top faculty members, another critical aspect of the Plan for Pre-eminence was overhauling the curriculum. One example was the school's real estate program. Some people on our Wharton board told us that MIT had a very strong program superior to ours. I told them we would develop the best real estate program at Wharton. We brought in some top faculty members, and then we also started building an advisory board of people from the industry. The reason we were able to attract these real estate businesspeople was that they not only wanted to come to seminars to find out the latest methods being used in the industry, but also wanted to get together and interact with other developers. We got the top people in real estate development to join us, and we made our real estate program the best in the country.

On my early visits to Wharton, I had observed that Wharton at that time had several programs that had developed around individuals rather than being part of the school's natural structure. For example, we had a program run by a distinguished professor of operations management. It had more than 100 Ph.D. candidates, many of whom did consulting much of the time. But the program had a conglomeration of people who didn't fit into any of the other disciplines, and I couldn't see how it fit into the school's overall Ph.D. program. Wharton had other similar centers run by people who had their own fiefdoms that had been built up over time. To an outsider like me, there appeared to be no rationale or rationality to some of these activities.

I strongly felt that we had to start clearing away those that did not seem to belong at Wharton. We simply did not have the time, money, or faculty to support all these programs—we had to concentrate on the programs that would have the greatest impact and that were part of the plan for pre-eminence. The biggest of these challenges was the operations management program that was also a huge consulting operation. Nobody dared touch this program because it was seen as being too powerful. The distinguished professor who ran it was a great academic and great consultant. But he just wanted to be left completely alone to run the program.

Not long after I became dean, the professor came to me and said he did not want to be the department chair anymore because he had too much to do. I agreed, and then he recommended another person to be the chair. My view was that that person could not be made chair because he was not a member of the tenured faculty. The professor insisted so I checked with the deputy dean for academic affairs, who agreed with me that department chairs had to be members of the tenured faculty. When I let the professor know it couldn't be done, he threatened to leave. I said, "We love you here and want you here, but that person is not going to be the department chair." So the professor left Wharton. This gave us the opening we needed. We shut down the program, allocated the faculty to various departments, and brought the Ph.D. students under the direction of the appropriate department. Remember the loose-brick theory I mentioned in the first chapter. In academia don't try to knock down the wall by charging ahead. You might break your neck. Wait for a brick to loosen and push it off. Six months before this it would have been impossible to shut down the program. Using the same principle, we also phased out many other programs that did not fit in with the overall mission of our strategic plan.

Energizing Executive Education

An important aspect of the plan for pre-eminence was to build an Executive Education program. One reason was that in addition to development, it was an important source of revenue. But in addition to the money, we also wanted exposure to the top companies and their executives. In the past, Wharton had minimal presence in Executive Education. A group went around and put on seminars in motels around the country, and we licensed the Wharton name to them. They used some Wharton professors, but we had no quality control over what they were doing. We shut down that program quickly.

When we proposed that we were going to do Executive Education as part of the plan for pre-eminence, the initial reaction from a large group of the professors—it was the most controversial part of our plan—was that they did not like it. The appropriate faculty committees had agreed we would do this. But some professors said that they already had the heaviest teaching load in the university, and that teaching executives was more than they could handle. I explained that any professor who did not want to teach in Executive Education would not have to do it. What I would have liked to tell them was that, probably, only 25% to 33% of them could teach in Executive Education anyway. I couldn't tell them that, but it was true. The students they would teach were not undergraduates or MBA candidates. These students were battle-hardened CEOs, COOs, and CFOs who had been out in the business world for some time and knew the way things worked. They would quickly know if a lecturer had his feet firmly planted in the real world of business or just had some theoretical ideas that might or might not work.

We decided to build the Steinberg Conference Center and the Aresty Institute for Executive Education. This program was a key strategic piece of our plan for pre-eminence. It accomplished several goals at the same time: bring money to the school to develop other programs, get in contact with a broad cross section of business executives, have the faculty learn from the executives as they are teaching them, and provide continuing education for alumni. Today it attracts more than 8,000 executives every year and brings in $50 million in revenues, at a very significant profit. The program is also ranked among the top executive education programs in the world.

Streamlining Fundraising

One of my major roles as Dean was to lead the school's fundraising effort. If we wanted to attract the best faculty members and increase faculty compensation, we needed money to do that. Virginia Clark, who is now head of development for the Smithsonian Institution, became the head of development and helped revamp the entire development area. At that time, the total budget of the school was around $50 million with only a small amount being provided by fundraising—and we needed much more.

Shortly after I arrived at Wharton, I got together with the development group and asked them, "How much money is each of you responsible for raising?"

They said, "That's not the way we do it."

"Well, how do you do it?"

"We go out and meet people, and we get them ready for the dean to see them and ask them for money."

"You mean everything depends on how much the dean can go around and do?" I asked. Apparently that was the case.

My view was different. I told the fundraisers that I believed they should all have goals, with each person responsible for bringing in a certain amount of money. They all turned pale. No way! They had never had the personal responsibility for raising any money. I added, "And then, if you meet your goals, I think you should get a bonus—a big bonus." Soon after that, about one-third of the people in development quit. They wanted no part of this new approach to fundraising. We had to replace another third, so we ended up with about a third of the people we had—and some more whom we hired.

So we set up fundraising goals, and we began to raise substantial amounts of money. When people met or exceeded their goals, as I had promised, we paid bonuses.

When the university heard we were paying bonuses to people who met their fundraising goals, the central fundraising group went ballistic. They asked who had authorized me to pay bonuses to fundraisers. The university had a lot of people doing fundraising, and they were not raising enough money. The university had a development group, as did Wharton, and both were supposed to work together and report to the university and to me. Well, I realized early that that system wasn't going to work, and for a very simple reason: The university's goal was contrary to Wharton's goal. The university's development group's goal was to divert as much money as possible from Wharton alumni—who had the most money—over to the university. Our job was to raise money for Wharton. These were not compatible goals.

The university's relationship with me was not acrimonious, but then it was not used to dealing with someone like me in the role. I just came in and said, "We are going to get certain things done. We don't want to harm the university. On the contrary, we have a responsibility to support and help the university. But correspondingly the university has a responsibility to enable us to attain our goals for Wharton." After all, a stronger Wharton would make for a stronger university.

Before we began the new approach to fundraising, Wharton was raising about $3 million a year. By the time I left seven years later, we were raising more than $30 million a year, and these days Wharton raises much more than that.

Working the Plan

After these elements of the plan for pre-eminence came together, we worked to achieve the goals—and we did that for the seven years I was at the school. We just kept attacking the plan. At every faculty meeting I would present how many new faculty members we had recruited, how much money we had raised, how many new student programs we had introduced, and so on. We tracked our performance against the plan. I used an early version of PowerPoint to present the results. The faculty members were terrific. People talk about the faculty being difficult to work with, but that isn't true; 90% were great. We also organized new boards. When I came in, we had one board of overseers. Then we added an undergraduate board, a graduate board, a real estate board, and so on. This allowed us to connect many executives to the Wharton School, and the school benefited in various ways from these relationships.

The Potential Pitfalls of Academic Leadership

More than half the people who come from outside academia to become deans of business schools do not succeed. The reason is not that they don't have an academic background; they just don't know how to deal with academics in a collegial fashion. Their approach to leadership in the business world often had been a "do it and do it now" attitude that I described in Chapter 3, "The Top-Down Organization: Learning That It's Not So Simple."

At Touche Ross I was used to dealing with 800 or 900 domestic partners, and many more from other countries. Though we couldn't run the firm like a true partnership, we had the trappings of a partnership and people believed they were partners. All the partners thought they were owners, and to make the system work, we had to be collegial consensus builders. For that reason, it wasn't as much of a transition for me to come into academia and make the faculty think they were the most important people, because the fact was they really were. I understood that I wasn't the most important person; I was a facilitator/leader. I could be their leader if they believed my aim was to help them get to where they wanted to go. Likewise, I could get my goals accomplished if they felt that generally they were getting what they wanted.

Businesspeople who have worked for "do it and do it now" kinds of organizations find it hard to understand this mindset. When they come into academia, they try to use the same approach that they used in the corporate world, and it doesn't work. It is because they fail to understand the context in which their leadership must operate.

Tom Ehrlich, who was provost at the University of Pennsylvania when I was Wharton's dean and then became the president of Indiana University, understands very well what it takes to lead effectively in academia. As he explains it, in academia it is important for the leader to know what to change as well as what to leave untouched. "Sometimes you just want to reinforce the culture, not just change it," he says. "No one in a university, for example, is going to change the overall culture of inquiry. It is a culture also of dispute—people challenging ideas. That is how knowledge is created, and untruths or lack of whole truths are exposed. You don't want to change that culture."

When Ehrlich moved from the University of Pennsylvania to Indiana University, he realized that he would have to bring about several changes. "The biggest barrier was inertia," he says. "The second was that lots of individuals could imagine that the changes I wanted to introduce would affect their activities adversely. The question that came to everyone's mind was, 'How am I going to be worse off because of this?' People were afraid that it would make vulnerable activities that did not have a marketplace justification, whereas in my view the opposite was true. It was my view that the institution should support activities for which there was no marketplace justification, but it should be very clear what the justification was. And some people were worried about that. As it was implemented, when budgets were tight, it is very easy to blame the new system, and when I was at the U Penn the system was always blamed. But we worked at it. The outcome was eventually much more positive than negative."

Leading in Other Contexts

Happily for successful academic leaders, their experience should serve them well whenever they find themselves in certain other contexts. The kind of collegial and collaborative leadership style that works with faculty and administrators should work equally well if you are appointed to outside commissions and committees—and even boards of directors. You will likely be thrown together with other leaders who will expect to have their say and a role in decision making. You have been through this already and should be able to contribute your own ideas and to share in the decision making without ruffling the feathers of your peers.

Hearing from the Faculty

I leave the final words to three Wharton faculty members who shed light on leadership in academia. Jerry Wind of the marketing department worked closely with me, and he chaired the search process for the dean before I came to Wharton. He says, "Don Carroll was a very entrepreneurial dean who had empowered the faculty, and during his tenure lots of centers flourished; but by the time he was ready to step down, the school needed a strong dean who could integrate various initiatives. We needed a leader who, in addition to being entrepreneurial, had two characteristics: first, someone who had the ability to deal with faculty, who could be prima donnas; and second, a person who would appreciate academic values. Russ Palmer had these characteristics. He was open to ideas, was not egocentric, had a warm personality, and had no hidden agendas. Most importantly, he was not a 'maintenance-type' dean—he was driven to make Wharton the number-one business school. We needed a leader, and with Palmer, that's what we got.

"The secret of Palmer's success at the school was that he realized that the plan for pre-eminence needed buy-in from various constituencies. He also believed in the KISS principle (keep it simple, stupid)—as demonstrated through the plan for pre-eminence. The plan had, in my mind, five simple elements:

1. Recruit the best faculty.
2. Retain and develop the best faculty.
3. Recruit the best students.
4. Get financial resources to pay for the above.
5. Develop key new programs, including Executive Education.

"He understood that academia is different than the corporate world," Wind continues. "In a company, the CEO's word is law. The CEO has much more power than a dean. In academia, the faculty members have tenure, while deans come and go. This leads to situations where often there is little time pressure. Things drag along. This makes leadership very difficult because the dean has little power over the faculty, especially the superstars, who tend to be prima donnas. These are people who would have 10 job offers if they made a single phone call. In addition, many faculty members don't care and don't want to be involved. They simply want to be left alone to pursue their research. This group needs to be energized. Yet another group—often including the superstars—tends to block progress. Finally, there is a group consisting of 10% to 20% of the faculty who care deeply about issues and who want to make things happen. Palmer's achievement was to energize this fourth group and to enlarge its base.

"One of the key things any dean has to realize is that while the dean can initiate some things (such as launching an Executive Education initiative), most other innovations in academia don't stem from the dean but from the fourth segment of the faculty. The dean's challenge is to empower this group and to make their activity consistent with his vision."

David Reibstein, also a professor of marketing, was at Wharton when I arrived. He says, "Initially I was not in favor of Russ Palmer's appointment as the dean. He was an accountant and a non-academic, and I was afraid he might not understand what a business school is all about. I was far from correct in my assessment.

"Palmer provided Wharton with a sense of direction—he listened to people and did it in a way that engaged people in the process of change. At one of our first faculty meetings, he gave an electronic presentation, lunch was provided, and [he] took attendance. He laid out a plan for the school. This was a huge cultural shift. Before that, there had not been a plan for the school.

"Palmer liked the word 'pre-eminent,'" Reibstein says. "He repeated it constantly—sometimes as many as 30 times in a presentation. But he didn't stop at that. He defined it, explained what was involved in the school becoming pre-eminent, what metrics should be used to track progress, and brought in outside auditors to evaluate us on our metrics. This made the school's mission clear to everyone. It injected energy and cohesiveness in the school—it rallied people around.

"Palmer faced tons of obstacles. These included a lethargic and unorganized faculty, and some faculty who thought they were in charge. Palmer was very likable, but he was not afraid to confront [powerful faculty] head-on when the need arose. He had very high integrity, and we knew where he stood on every issue.

"Palmer knew what he wanted and how to get it. He wanted me to be the deputy dean. I said no, because I was planning to take a sabbatical. He asked me, 'What would it take for you to be interested in the deputy dean's position?' Those were among his favorite lines...'What would it take?' and 'Let's make it happen.' He used that approach constantly to recruit talented faculty members and bring them to Wharton."

The other faculty member is Michael Useem, professor of management who arrived after I had left, and now is Director of the Center for Leadership and Change Management. "When I joined Wharton in 1991, Russ Palmer had already left—but he left a footprint that was visible long after he left the school," Useem says. "The school had momentum, optimism, and it was growing aggressively—and that was Palmer's doing. These were like the archaeological artifacts of his impact on Wharton.

"I did not hear a single critical observation about Palmer after I joined the school. It's akin to what people said about George C. Marshall; he was such a gentleman that no one could criticize him to his face or behind his back. That is an important aspect of leadership.

"Leadership in academia is particularly difficult because the criteria for performance are vague and ambiguous," Useem says. "In addition, the dean's ability to make changes is often nonexistent because of tenured faculty. That gives a dean very limited ability to control the most important resource—people. Faculty members are like solo entrepreneurs, self-directing and focused on their own projects. That makes it very difficulty for any leader to succeed in academia.

"How is success determined in academia? First, it takes strong academic credentials, which Palmer did not have. To lead a hospital, you need an M.D., and to be accepted as a leader in academia, you need a Ph.D., though such credentials are often paper-deep. Second, you need an exquisite ability to appreciate value drivers. Third, you have to be a very quick study; you need to be fast on the uptake.

"My sense is that Palmer may not have had academic credentials," Useem continues, "but he overcame that obstacle in a way that you can still physically feel his legacy. He did it by putting a huge premium on results. That is what gave him his spinal strength. He made Wharton focus on what drives academic reputation and academic performance.

"Palmer's performance at his first faculty meeting—where he got the faculty's attention by changing his message to focus on compensation—offers four leadership lessons. The first is that leaders always feel their audience. Palmer was not just giving a speech—he was also reading his audience. Great actors have this ability. Second, he didn't stick with his prepared speech. At the risk of causing consternation, he altered his message. Third, you have to have the ability to say what you say so that it sticks. Flexibility is crucial. Improv offers good training for leadership. Broadway doesn't prepare you for leadership as much as Saturday Night Live. Finally, when you change a message, you need to follow through. If you can't deliver, the result is worse than saying nothing at all. But Palmer did follow through, with results that we can still see today."

Summary

- To lead in academia, you need to begin by recognizing that a collegial culture is very different from corporate culture. A dean in a business school cannot assume that his or her word is law. Faculty have tenure, whereas deans come and go. As a result, decisions are often made by consensus and can take a very long time to make. Failure to understand this reality has tripped up many business leaders who have tried to make the transition to academic leadership.

- It follows from the culture described previously that in academia, trying to bring about change all at once is generally likely to lead to frustration. You must wait for a brick to loosen, and then push it out.

- As in other contexts, if you want to succeed as a leader in academia, you must understand the needs—both articulated and unarticulated—of your constituents. This means understanding, first and foremost, the needs of the faculty, but also those of other constituents such as students, alumni, corporate donors, and recruiters, among others. You must formulate and articulate a collective vision that is as much as possible based on understanding the needs of these constituents.

- After the vision has been established and a program has been built around it, you need to pursue it with vigor without being frustrated or thwarted by academic bureaucrats. Integrity is crucial in gaining the support of different constituents.

- Although it is important to be collegial and transparent, this does not mean that you blindly acquiesce to every whim and fancy of faculty members. If an academic program does not fit with the overall mission, you can't shy away from challenging and confronting programs whose purpose is questionable. Shutting down such programs can free up valuable resources that can be put to better use.

- When goals are achieved, you should reward those who contribute to realizing the vision.

Chapter 9

NATIONAL CULTURES AND CONTEXT: LEADING IN A GLOBAL ENVIRONMENT

Today's firms are increasingly operating in a global system of interrelated businesses. Many have expanded their businesses by buying and selling their products and services internationally; an increasing number of others now operate full businesses in many—sometimes more than 100—countries. In either case, leaders will have to understand the national cultures in which they are doing business if they are to succeed. In this chapter, I discuss how a leader's ability to execute is deeply influenced by the culture and society in which the organization itself operates. What followers expect of their leaders and the traits that make leaders effective vary across different societies and cultures. Leaders cannot afford to take a one-size-fits-all approach toward society and culture. Our world is simply too diverse.

I begin by describing experiences I had working with companies that operate in very different cultures from our own. This raises the question of whether there are global principles of leadership that apply to all cultures, and I discuss those that I believe are universal. Then I combine my own experience with real-life experiences and research of others and describe a number of major national cultures you are likely to encounter in today's "flat world." I point to the example of Honeywell, which has done a tremendous job in setting up a program that can help its executives manage across national borders, and then I conclude with the pitfalls that await if you are unprepared to understand national differences.

Context: Diverse National Cultures

I begin with a personal experience that gives a vivid sense of the potential perils and eventual success of working in a very different national culture. While I was CEO of Touche Ross, we saw an opportunity to expand our business in the oil-rich Middle East. The predominant accounting firm in the Arab League countries was Saba & Co. Fuad S. Saba (or FSS, as he was called) had founded the firm in 1926, but by the 1970s it was run by his son Suhail. Headquartered in Beirut since 1948, the Saba firm had offices all over the Middle East. Earlier Saba had been associated with Arthur Andersen, but for whatever reason, that relationship was coming to an end in the late 1970s. We had heard that Arthur Andersen had wanted everything done the "U.S. way." When word spread that Saba was breaking with Arthur Andersen, essentially every other member of the Big Eight accounting firms wanted to sign up Saba to join their organization.

Touche Ross was then the smallest of the Big Eight, and since we had no oil companies as clients, we could probably have given Saba the least amount of U.S.-related work. But Touche Ross International wanted to build its presence in the Middle East, so I called up Suhail Saba and told him I wanted to meet him. He asked where we wanted to meet, and I said we would go to Beirut. "Wouldn't you like to meet in Cyprus or someplace else?" he asked. I replied that since their offices were in Beirut, that's where we would go.

Three colleagues and I planned to go to Beirut for the meeting. The first thing we did was find out how much it would cost us to insure our lives for $1 million each for three days, and Lloyd's of London came back with a quote of $80,000. The reason for this high quote was that it was 1978, and a war was raging in Lebanon. Eventually we were able to buy insurance for a lower price and we flew to Beirut. We landed at the airport, and as we went down the stairs, I saw that an armored limousine and a guard with a machine gun were waiting to take us to the meeting. When we reached the hotel, we were told to keep the curtains pulled in our rooms. Someone did get shot while standing on a balcony while we were there. But it did not happen in our building; it happened a couple of buildings away. We went out for dinner that evening to a different hotel. It was the only structure standing on that street. All the others were pockmarked with bullets and had been demolished by bombs.

We met the next day with Suhail Saba and his top partners; they decided, shortly thereafter, to join Touche Ross International. The main reason was that we had gone to Beirut. No other firm would meet with them there—they all wanted to meet in Cyprus or London or some place that was less dangerous. The fact that we were willing to go to the place where they were doing business every day to talk to them was the prime reason they joined us. It touched them deeply that we had done that. "You are the kind of people we want to do business with," they said.

That was the only reason why we were able to bring the Saba firm into the Touche Ross fold; we couldn't offer them as much business as Price Waterhouse or Coopers & Lybrand could. That shows you how important personal relationships are in most cultures. We also gave them a great deal of autonomy and did not look down on the way they did business from a cultural standpoint, and that helped us strengthen the relationship further. They were a firm of high integrity and principles. I never heard of them paying people off or any practices like that, but the Middle Eastern business standards were different.

This experience illustrates how important it is to tailor your approach to working with people in different cultures. It does not mean that what we did will work in every culture. For instance, an egalitarian, consensus-building approach may be seen as a positive leadership trait in some cultures, but in others it could well be viewed as failure to "manage" and provide direction, and thus be interpreted by followers as a sign of weakness. This leads me to address the question of whether any leadership principles are universal.

The truth is, most of the principles of leadership I mentioned in Chapter 1, "Leadership Principles: The Basis of Successful Leadership," are universal, but they are practiced differently in different parts of the world. Consider, for example, personal integrity, which is the foundation of leadership. I believe that integrity and leadership go together all over the world; I cannot imagine people in different parts of the world accepting a person without integrity as a leader over a long period. Idi Amin, Adolph Hitler, Benito Mussolini, Saddam Hussein—all these people played leadership roles, but eventually they came to a bad end. You might go astray from the principles of leadership, but in time it catches up with you. The *basic principles* of leadership are universal.

Perhaps someone may point to Switzerland and say, although I talk about openness and transparency being important leadership principles, look how secretive people are in that country. I have dealt with Swiss bankers, and you can spend a long time talking to them and wonder in the end what they really told you. But ultimately, people have to trust their bankers. If they don't trust them, they are not going to do business with them.

That is why I believe the basic principles of leadership are universal, although, as I have said, they are applied differently in different parts of the world. Take the Japanese, whom some people regard as inscrutable or mysterious. In my interactions with them, I learned that after you have developed a personal relationship with them, you can count on them to do what they say. I have found in my dealings with Japanese executives that when someone has personally agreed to do something, he or she can be trusted.

Good judgment is another attribute of a good leader—and that is true universally. Other universal principles are the ability to build confidence in followers by setting high expectations and then ensuring that followers develop the confidence to meet those expectations, and the ability to understand the goals, desires, wants, and needs of followers and to help them achieve these goals. It's also universally true that leaders make the difference in performance. Good leaders elicit good performance and poor leaders don't.

As opposed to these underlying principles, the style of leadership has to be different in various cultures. Japanese society, for example, has a great reverence for age. Young people may come along, and though they may be very bright and talented, Japanese society generally regards them as potential leaders who may reach leadership roles in the future but are not there yet. That is not the case in the U.S. Most Americans believe that the young bucks of Silicon Valley or relatively young executives like Bill Gates have the leadership ability to change the world.

Americans, however, should not be tempted to expect to dictate our business practices and customs in different parts of the world any more than we can expect to impose our form of democracy on Iraq, Iran, or Afghanistan. These customs and cultures have developed in many cases over more than a thousand years. How can we believe that we can—or even should—change all this overnight? We should first clean up some of the practices in City Hall or in Congress, and for that matter, in parts of the business world, before we feel we are the shining example for others to emulate.

Taking a broader look at national differences, I argue that leadership and business are not very different from what we read in the newspapers every day about foreign affairs. The U.S. can almost always count on the UK, for example. Why? To some extent the reasons are cultural, but it also often serves the interests of the UK to support the U.S. In the same way, the U.S. can almost always count on France to say the Americans are doing something wrong. Again, to some extent it's cultural—the cards are stacked against the U.S. because many people in France regard Americans as boorish cowboys who don't understand the world or how it works. What makes a difference when we go from the world's political structures down to business? Self-interest and personal relationships. When it is in the self-interest of other countries to support what the U.S. is doing, they do so. When it's not in their self-interest, they go their own way. And so it is in business.

The lessons about self-interest and the importance of personal relationships were brought home to me many times while I was CEO of Touche Ross. These two factors helped us maintain business relationships between the U.S. firm and our partner firms in other countries. We could cater to the self-interest of foreign firms by providing them with business that they could not generate for themselves, and they could provide us with opportunities that we could not tap on our own. Also we could provide new products and educational opportunities. We also built strong personal relationships with international firms that resulted in relationships of trust.

However, if you think about it, this is a pretty fragile structure because these relationships could change. One of our competitors could come along to one of our international partner firms and say, "You've got X amount of referral business from the U.S., but we'll give you double that." Or they could schmooze with the leaders of our partner firms, take them out to dinner, offer them positions on international committees or boards, and do things that generally undermined our personal relationship. That did happen, and we did lose some partner firms that way. Only a few, but we kept most of them.

The point to remember is that cultural differences run deep. You not only have to accept them, but also have to acknowledge them. You have to treat people so they know that you do not in any way believe you are superior to them. If anything, you almost need to treat them as if they are superior to you. You have to make them think that their country is great—because it really is—and that the meeting their firm has organized is a most spectacular one. You have to tell them how important they are, send them notes, dance with their wives at firm dinners, and do what you need to do to maintain your relationship. If they don't think they can trust you on a personal level, you are in big trouble.

Before I present some empirical research on leadership, and a systematic examination of specific national cultures that was developed at Touche Ross, I want to describe several more experiences I had at the firm to emphasize the variety of cultures you are likely to encounter. Touche Ross had an affiliate firm in the Philippines. I was warned that this firm had been bribing tax authorities on behalf of their domestic clients. This was illegal so I said we ought to find another affiliate. But that was a problem. When we asked around, we were told that this was a common practice among most of the independent accounting firms in the Philippines. One exception was the SGV Group headed by Wash SyCip, but they already served several firms in the Big Eight. Eventually we ended up starting our own firm. But this experience helped us understand that this is how business was being done in that part of the world. After we had our own firm, we were able to serve our U.S. clients or German clients in that country, but obviously we did not get a whole lot of local business from clients who expected us to follow the local practices. Even if you are operating in an environment of questionable practices, it's essential that you maintain the integrity issue between yourself and your associates. Fundamentally, if you act with integrity, they will believe that they can trust you.

Personal relationships were important in other parts of the world, and we were sensitive to how to adapt them to specific cultures. In Japan, we had a good working relationship with Tohmatsu Awoki & Co., though it was not part of Touche Ross International in the initial stages. Still, it was the Japanese accounting firm with which everyone wanted to do business. We had talked to the head of the firm on several occasions about becoming a member of our firm and working on an exclusive basis. I had developed a pretty good personal relationship with the managing partner, Iwao Tomita. In 1975, we invited him to Williamsburg for our big international meeting. This was where the heads of Touche Ross firms from 80 countries came, mostly with their spouses. We had a good meeting and then it was time for the final-night dinner. During the dinner I went to Tomita-san and asked if we could meet privately. We went to an adjacent room and I said, "Do you know something that would be totally spectacular if we did it here tonight?" When he asked what I had in mind, I said, "It would be great if we announced that Tohmatsu Awoki has joined Touche Ross International. We could go out right now and tell everybody here and it would be a tremendous surprise and you would be a hero."

We talked over a few issues, and then he said, "Okay." Just like that. We went back to the dining room to announce it. We stopped the band, got up on the stage, and said, "We want to tell you something terrific and we know you are going to be as thrilled about it as we are. Tonight, Tohmatsu Awoki has joined Touche Ross." As we had expected, cheers and loud applause followed. Eventually, the firm's international name was changed to what it still is today—Deloitte Touche Tohmatsu. Tohmatsu Awoki is now the largest accounting firm in Japan. It never would have happened without three things: a history of careful cultivation of our personal relationship with Iwao Tomita that convinced him of our integrity; a win-win situation financially; and sealing the deal at the right moment.

To be sure, our partner firms joined us out of self-interest as well. But even when we could not offer the best business deal, they did ultimately get what they wanted from the association. But the most important reason was that they valued the relationship we had with them and they believed in our integrity. That is what made it work.

If there is one point that I would emphasize above all others about the experience of building Touche Ross International globally, it is that while our competitors staffed their overseas offices mainly with Americans, we took the opposite approach. The bedrock of our international firm was local leaders, not U.S. expatriates whom we sent overseas. We took this approach because we had to do it; we really had no other choice because we were the youngest firm and coming into the global game late. We did not want to change their business culture or impose our ideas upon them; we wanted local leaders to come up and actively work with us in building our global enterprise, making it truly an international not a U.S. firm. We would help them with training and with finding clients, but trusted them to be our equals in every respect. The approach we took with the Saba firm in the Middle East and other firms in different parts of the world reflected this international policy. That was what made Touche Ross International's approach different at that time from that of other firms, and it turned out to be our greatest global strategic advantage.

With these real-world examples as background, I now turn to the work of academics who have studied leadership in the international arena.

Culture and Leadership Styles: The GLOBE Project

In 1993, Wharton Management Professor Robert House "launched The Global Leadership and Organizational Behavior Effectiveness Research Program (GLOBE) to test leadership hypotheses in various cultures," as reported in *Knowledge@Wharton*, the online research and business analysis journal of the Wharton School.[1] As the article states, over time GLOBE "evolved into a multi-phase, multi-method research project in which some 170 investigators from more than 60 cultures representing all major regions of the world collaborated to examine the interrelationships among societal culture, organizational culture and practices and organizational leadership. GLOBE focused on universals and culture-based differences in perceived effectiveness of leadership attributes by asking middle managers whether certain leader characteristics and behaviors would help or hinder a person in becoming an outstanding leader." This approach would ensure a systematic and reliable understanding of the differences in leadership styles in diverse national cultures.

Interestingly, as I have argued previously, House and his colleagues found that "there are universally endorsed leader attributes. In addition," the article continues, "the study also found that there are attributes that are universally seen as impediments to outstanding leadership. The most important finding, however, is that there are culturally-contingent attributes that can help or hinder leadership. What is seen as a strength in one culture may be a considerable impediment in another culture."

House and his colleagues noted that to "see how cultures might come into play, we can easily imagine a situation in which a British executive who was trained at an American business school is asked to run the Argentine manufacturing facility of a Japanese firm. What leadership attributes should this executive work to develop: Japanese? Argentine? American? British? This executive needs to understand the culture within which he works and how his employees perceive leadership. An executive needs to develop leadership attributes, tailored to the unique culture within which he or she works."

The article makes the point that the GLOBE project showed that "different cultural groups may vary in their conceptions of the most important characteristics of charismatic/transformational leadership. In some cultures, one might need to take strong, decisive action in order to be seen as a leader, while in other cultures consultation and a democratic approach may be the preferred approach to exercising effective leadership." In studying management practices, the researchers found that "many attributes associated with charisma are seen as contributing to outstanding leadership, but the term 'charisma' invokes ambivalence in several countries. There is concern in some cultures that people tend to lose their balance and perspective as a result of an excessive focus on achievement created by charismatic leaders. Certainly the most notorious example of a charismatic leader is Hitler."

The researchers also found that seemingly universal leadership qualities such as vision and risk taking carry considerable cultural baggage. "Leaders are expected to have vision, but how this is displayed differs from culture to culture," the article says. "In China, the influence of Confucian values makes people wary of leaders who talk without engaging in specific action. Indian managers, on the other hand, care less about visionaries, preferring bold assertive styles of leadership. Leaders are often thought to be risk takers, but GLOBE found that risk taking is not universally valued as contributing to outstanding leadership."

Communication skills are extremely important for leaders, but what "constitutes a good communicator is likely to vary greatly across cultures," the article points out. "American managers are more likely to provide directions to subordinates on a face-to-face basis while Japanese managers are likely to use written memos. In the U.S., subordinates are usually provided negative feedback directly from their supervisors, while in Japan such feedback is usually channeled through a peer of the subordinates. These differences reflect the U.S. individualistic norm of 'brute honesty' and the Japanese collectivistic norm of 'face-saving.'"

Now I offer the example of Honeywell, a company that I think is doing a good job of recruiting and developing executives to manage across different national cultures. David M. Cote, the company's chairman and CEO, offers outstanding principles and practical advice in this regard.

Building Global Leaders: The Honeywell Way

Honeywell, as noted in an earlier chapter, is a manufacturer with revenues of $31 billion. The company's operations span the globe. It has been doing business in the Asia Pacific region for more than 70 years; for example, it has been licensing manufacturing products in Japan since the 1930s. Its Asian operations are headquartered in Singapore, from where the company oversees operations in 13 countries including Australia and the Asian nations of India, China, Korea, and Taiwan, among others. More than 13,000 employees work for Honeywell in the Asia Pacific region. In addition, the company has a strong manufacturing base in Europe, the Middle East, and Africa. These operations are managed from regional headquarters in Brussels, and they involve 25,000 employees who work for Honeywell establishments in 49 European, African, or Middle Eastern countries. Moreover, Honeywell has affiliates in 10 Latin American countries including Argentina, Brazil, Chile, Colombia, and Ecuador, among others. The company has more than 7,000 employees in Latin America.

Given its global footprint, how does Honeywell train its executives to be successful leaders in different parts of the world? The company employs a program called the "12 behaviors," according to David M. Cote, the company's present Chairman and Chief Executive. "We created it about five years ago to lay out what we expect of all Honeywell employees and particularly from Honeywell leadership," he says. "During the annual appraisal process, everyone gets measured on those 12 behaviors." Cote explains that the reason the 12 behaviors program is significant is that when Honeywell recruits people in different parts of the world, it employs those who will fit the 12 behaviors best. "In other words, we don't hire them first and then train them in those behaviors; we hire them based on their ability to work in conjunction with these behaviors," he says.

For example, one of the behaviors is teamwork. "It is an overused word. After all, who would not be in favor of teamwork?" Cote asks. "But it is not always well understood, because teamwork sometimes implies that everyone must agree." Honeywell, however, defines teamwork in a specific way: The company sets out the requirements of a team member and specifies how these differ from those of a team leader.

If an issue is being discussed, it is incumbent upon team members to speak up and express their opinion and to make sure that their point of view is heard. "If, after being heard, the decision goes against you, it is up to you to support that decision," Cote says. "Your point was heard, but once the decision is made, you have to support it." In contrast, a team leader is required to ensure that members speak up when an issue is being discussed. "You cannot just expect that people will speak up willingly," Cote says. "It is not just a cultural issue; it is also a personal issue. Extroverted people tend to speak up, and introverted people do not; and unless called on specifically they may not speak up at all." Cote explains that it is also incumbent upon the team leader to make a decision. He or she cannot just sit there and wait for consensus. "It is incumbent upon the leader to get the facts and opinions and then make a decision. There are some times when leaders can ask for more data, but then they must be able to make a timely call."

This is precisely an area where differences in cultural or social context could lead to different behaviors. Whereas in countries like the U.S. people might be willing to speak up openly, in many Asian cultures dissent within a team might be regarded as being disrespectful of the leader or even as being insubordinate. How does Honeywell train its team leaders to manage teams in such contexts?

Cote's answer is that this is why hiring people who fit the 12 behaviors is important. Cote says: "If I am told that people in India or China will not speak up to disagree at team meetings, my response is that no people in any country are all the same. They are not. You only need to find 2,000 or 3,000 people out of more than a billion people in India who are predisposed to thinking this way." Cote adds that sometimes "more issues are made of cultural differences than are really there. I firmly believe that all people want to be treated with basic respect and courtesy and recognition that they and their country are of value. That is not hard to do."

Cote recognizes, of course, that in some cultures authoritarian leaders are treated with respect rather than being resented: "If you try to hire people in South Korea, you tend to find people who are autocratic leaders, and employees who expect an autocratic leader. However, we have also learned that when you put someone there who is more team-based, instead of laying down the law about how they expect things to work, most people seem to get there. That is why it is not right to stereotype a country. All the people are not like that." This is also true of the U.S., Cote adds. "We may say that people tend to speak up, but the fact is that extroverted people tend to speak up. But there are also a lot of introverted people in the U.S., and until you ask them directly, you are probably not going to get their opinion."

As the leader of a company with operations in more than 70 countries, Cote regularly conducts town hall meetings around the world for audiences ranging from 100 to 2,000 people. He has conducted at least 40 meetings outside the U.S., and in almost every country he has visited, he has been told not to be surprised if no one asks questions at the end of his presentation. According to local experts, "Our culture is just not like that." And yet, Cote says, "in not one case has there been a problem with people asking questions. What it comes down to is, what kind of an environment do you set up upfront, and how do you make people feel comfortable asking questions. You find that the experts—the communications people—are wrong."

Cote offers another example of the problem that stereotypes can create: "In the UK we had to move a plant from one location to another, and we had decided to offer packages to people who agreed to move." Cote was warned not to expect a high response because "nobody moves in the UK." Cote asked the local Honeywell executives, "How do you know if you don't offer the packages? Why don't you make the offer and see what happens?" When the offer was made, Honeywell's British executives were astonished to see that large numbers of people accepted the packages and agreed to move. "They said they liked what they did, and they agreed to move for the job. People get too hung up on their stereotypes."

Laughter: The Best Medicine

Cote also believes that if the leader has a sense of humor, it goes a long way toward bridging cultural gaps. "No matter what culture you go to, people have a sense of humor. If you can find some way to tap into that sense of humor, so that it's not just completely serious, you can make progress. It's one of those universal truths about people."

One time, Cote was involved with negotiations in Japan with people whom he had not dealt with before. In the beginning of the conversation, he began to joke about cultural differences involving food. "I talked about how I preferred a cheeseburger to a traditional Japanese bento box, and then I started teasing them about why we couldn't have a cheeseburger bento box. Everyone laughed, and as we did that, we started to develop a rapport. Then the negotiations began, and we ended up in a tough spot. Both sides knew it was a tough issue, and finally the Japanese executives said yes. Then I said, 'We were talking about this before. There are cultural differences—so, is this a Japanese yes or an American yes? I'm wondering which one this is.' Again, everyone smiled and laughed, and then we went on to discuss the issue even further until it was resolved. The point is that there are cultural differences, and you have to recognize them; but as long as you have basic respect for people—and you use a sense of humor—that can get you through a lot of situations."

Even as Cote recognizes that cultural and social contexts differ around the world, he acknowledges that there are some universal principles that people need in order to become successful leaders anywhere. "You need integrity," he says. "No matter what culture you belong to, people need to be able to trust you. If you are a leader, you have to be able to do what we call integrative thinking. You must be able to pick all the different pieces of what people are telling you, and manage to contrive an answer or solution that addresses the problem. You have to be able to pick little pieces from what a lot of people are saying and form a mosaic that clarifies the picture. Those are some of the key principles."

A Tool for Success: The 80-20 Rule

How should companies prepare leaders who have been successful in one part of the world become effective leaders in a different region and culture? Cote says he has found that moving from one part of the world to another is "analogous to moving from one business to another in the same country. When you look at cultural differences, they exist between different countries but also within different companies and sometimes even within different businesses in the same company."

Cote suggests that the way to deal with such change is to use what he calls his "80-20 rule: 80% of what you deal with in the new situation is exactly the same as what you have dealt with in the past, and you have to deal with it the same way; 20% is different. The people I have seen fail—when they change companies or businesses or countries—are those who go in saying that since they did things a certain way in the past, they will do it the same way again, or those who think they are in a totally new situation and nothing of what they have learned in the past is applicable. Both of those are failure modes. The person who is in success mode walks in saying, 'I know it's 80-20. My trick is to figure out what's in the 80 (and I should do it exactly the way I did before) and what's in the 20 (and I need to modify my way of working to comply with the new company, or country).'"

These principles—and practical advice—from the Honeywell chairman can go a long way in helping leaders of all organizations manage more effectively across different national and social contexts.

Characteristics of Some Major National Cultures

Tom Presby, who worked with me at Touche Ross, has spent a good part of his life doing business globally. Here are his empirical observations on certain national cultures as a rough guide to what you can expect when working in these countries. Though they may sound like cultural stereotypes, they are based on his personal experience.

Latin-Based Europe (France, Spain, Italy, French Belgium, French Switzerland)

a. Elegance is an important aspect of their approach to transactions, business arrangements, and life in general. This can seem like a complicating factor and can result in convoluted transactions when more straightforward solutions could be possible.

b. Honor and pride trump pragmatic solutions. Executives are sometimes willing to forego achieving a monetary goal if it means compromising their view of their honor or pride.

c. Unlike many other cultures where a calm exterior is important, people get angry all the time, but it's generally just a transaction and not necessarily a fracture in a relationship.

d. Social standing counts. This can stem from either family or successful completion of education at an elite university.

e. People tend to be very loyal to personal friendships.

f. Tax minimization schemes (sometimes illegal ones) are often employed.

Germanic European Countries (Germany, Austria, Flemish Belgium)

a. People are very conservative about change and particularly attached to doing all things "the German way," which is thought to be superior in every aspect.

b. Their approach to business is hierarchical based on position and university diploma. This makes collaboration and teamwork difficult.

c. They are formal in their approach to doing business, business relationships, contracts, regulations, and so forth.

d. They may not be as scrupulous as their formal approach might suggest.

Scandinavia/Netherlands/Luxembourg/Belgium (*to Some Extent*)

a. People take a pragmatic approach to business.

b. They are egalitarian in work relationships and in compensation, resulting in many relatively flat compensation arrangements within (even large) enterprises.

c. Once a relationship has been established and trust has been earned, they are loyal.

d. They are obsessed with escaping taxation.

United Kingdom

a. They are the ultimate pragmatists.

b. They are ambivalent about being part of Europe. In fact, they can use this to their advantage. When it suits them to be European, they highlight their ties to the EU and the Continent. When it does not, they highlight their historic separation and their refusal to join the Monetary System.

c. For them, social standing counts. Family counts most, followed by schooling.

d. Despite the hierarchical nature of most of their enterprises, they are capable of teamwork.

e. They can be loyal friends and business partners.

Japan

a. "Face" counts most. Never suggest in public or in private that a Japanese person is wrong or has made a mistake.

b. Trust is the key to relationships. Trust must be earned by persistence and by showing respect for Japanese institutions.

c. They are generally loyal, once trust has been established.

d. They make good partners, and generally deliver on commitments.

e. They are often incapable of taking public, negative action against other Japanese people or institutions.

Russia

a. Corruption is commonplace. It does not stem from a person's decision to transgress from proper and honest behavior; it is simply the way normal business gets done.

b. Most people hold the belief that business is a sort of zero-sum game; that is, to earn a profit means taking it away from someone else. The concept of growing a financially successful enterprise that adds to the economy, pays its employees properly, and earns profits for its owners is an extremely difficult concept to grasp.

c. The generations are very different from one another. People who held management positions under the pre-1990 regime are hopeless in terms of adapting to market capitalism. People who graduated from universities during the 1990s met with the chaos of the times. Very few were exposed to properly run and successful businesses. The newest generation has been exposed to successful businesses during the Putin years and often in the Putin management style.

d. The country is full of young, attractive, well-educated, multilingual Russians. If they were educated in Russia, outsiders should be careful about trusting them with information and/or responsibility.

e. There is little loyalty to a company or enterprise, whether foreign or Russian owned.

f. Negotiations never stop until (and sometimes after) documents are signed. The classic "handshake agreement" has little meaning.

g. Don't rely on Russian courts for justice or Russian lawyers for advice. Deals should be structured accordingly.

h. Management style is hierarchical as opposed to collaborative. Rank is still measured by how many people a manager supervises—a holdover from former times.

i. East–West joint ventures generally fail. Make sure to include a buyout provision.

j. Notwithstanding all the above, it is possible to build a successful business with a largely Russian management and staff.

Former Soviet Europe

a. Even though many East European countries have already joined the EU, they still have certain characteristics similar to Russia (described previously).

b. Perhaps the biggest distinction between the former Soviet satellites in Europe and Russia itself is that the Europeans did have a background in market-based economies and democratic societies a few generations ago. These roots come out in the legal systems and business instincts of the people.

It is impossible to describe all the national cultures you can encounter in the global marketplace. The footnote references at the end of the chapter provide a guide to further reading that can help you adapt to a wide range of specific national cultures.

Before turning to the pitfalls of failing to take into account the different national cultures, I want to qualify the discussion so far. There is no such thing as a completely uniform national culture. Yes, there are certain characteristics that are shared by a large number of people in different cultures. But when you are working with specific groups, you will find significant variations among individuals. Some will be active and aggressive and others will be passive and quiet, no matter what wider culture they live in. Your task is to adjust your leadership style in such a way that you take into account these differences and bring out the best that each has to offer your strategic objective.

Now we will turn to two examples of what could happen if leaders ignore national contexts in managing their operations.

The Potential Pitfalls of Leading in Diverse National Cultures

In their book *The Transplanted Executive: Why You Need to Understand How Workers in Other Countries See the World Differently*,[2] Professors P. Christopher Earley and Miriam Erez cite the instance of CTX, a high-tech printing equipment maker headquartered in Israel, which ran into great difficulties because of the failure of Israeli executives to communicate effectively with their overseas subsidiaries. The company made its equipment in Israel, and the subsidiaries were expected to provide service and maintenance in their respective countries. The subsidiaries were required to provide daily reports about service and maintenance issues, which they often failed to do. In frustration, the general manager in Israel invited the managers of all subsidiaries to attend a communications workshop at headquarters. The Israeli general manager began by lashing out at executives from the subsidiaries for not filing their reports, and added that he would give them two minutes to explain their failure to do so. The European managers were both offended and outraged at this treatment, and the communication problem worsened instead of improving, as the Israeli leaders had hoped.

The reason that the cure was worse, in a sense, than the disease had to do with the cultural nuances that underlay these communications. In Israel, many managers develop a forceful, authoritarian style as a result of that country's compulsory military service and other factors—and Israeli workers, who are used to this culture, not only do not feel offended by such behavior but generally see it as a sign of strength and decisiveness. In contrast, the European managers interpreted the Israelis' behavior as being domineering and offensive—and they responded by refusing to submit their reports. As the authors observe, the European "cultural values were similar to but not identical to the Israelis'."

According to the authors, companies need to use an integrated approach to managing cultural values if they want to overcome such challenges.

CTX is hardly alone. Wal-Mart, the Arkansas-based retail giant that has risen to the top of the Fortune 500 list, offers among the best examples of a company that failed to execute its strategy because it could not navigate cultural currents effectively. After nearly 10 years of trying to establish a strong retail brand in Germany, Wal-Mart left Germany in the summer of 2006.

In an article analyzing the reasons for Wal-Mart's failure, the *New York Times* noted, "Some of Wal-Mart's problems stem from hubris, a uniquely powerful American enterprise trying to impose its values around the world. In particular, Wal-Mart's experience in Germany, where it lost hundreds of millions of dollars since 1998, has become a sort of template for how not to expand into a country."[3]

The article quoted Beth Keck, an international spokeswoman for Wal-Mart, who said that that the company's experience in Germany was "a good, important lesson, a turning point." She said that the company had been naive in its approach to other countries and that, "Germany was a good example of that naïvete." The *New York Times* article continued, "Wal-Mart is also trying to integrate acquisitions with more sensitivity—a process that involves issues like deciding whether to consolidate multiple foreign headquarters and how aggressively to impose Wal-Mart's corporate culture on non-American employees" For example, "in Germany, Wal-Mart stopped requiring sales clerks to smile at customers—a practice that some male shoppers interpreted as flirting—and scrapped the morning Wal-Mart chant by staff members."

When a giant like Wal-Mart stumbles in failing to understand a major national culture, we should be doubly warned about this kind of pitfall.

Summary

- Just as success in execution depends upon your ability to understand and navigate through an organizational context, it also depends on understanding national cultures and social context. You cannot hope to be effective if you use a one-size-fits-all model of leadership everywhere.

- The principles of leadership are mainly universal, but the way in which you should apply them depends on the cultural context.

- Cultural differences run deep. You not only have to accept them, but also have to acknowledge them by treating people accordingly. People in different cultures must come to know that you do not in any way believe you are superior to them. If anything, you almost need to treat them as if they are superior to you.

- The perils of not understanding national cultures can include complete business failure in that culture.

Endnotes

1 *Knowledge@Wharton*, "How Cultural Factors Affect Leadership," July 23, 1999. Available online at: http://knowledge.wharton.upenn.edu/article.cfm? articleid=38. Requires that you sign up for the *Knowledge@Wharton* online journal.

2 Earley, P. Christopher, and Miriam Erez. *The Transplanted Executive: Why You Need to Understand How Workers in Other Countries See the World Differently* (New York: Oxford University Press, 1997), pp. 5-7. The authors provide an interesting table of Cultural Profiles with Example[s of]Management Practice, listing many countries, p. 27.

3 Mark Landler and Michael Barbaro, "No, Not Always" (International Business), *New York Times*, August 2, 2006. The article describes a number of the gaffes that Wal-Mart committed in attempting to impose its successful American system in Germany.

The Wider View of Leadership

After describing a wide range of contexts that leaders are likely to find themselves in, I need to add one more essential variable. This is the absolute necessity to motivate your workers. A carefully crafted strategic plan may have been drafted and task forces organized to carry it out, but unless the troops are eager to begin to renew the organization according to plan, it's almost certain to face possible failure or be implemented marginally no matter what the context. So in Chapter 10, I describe ways of motivating workers.

In Chapter 11, I return to the principles of leadership and describe how they can differ in application depending on different contexts.

Chapter 10

THE HEART OF LEADERSHIP: MOTIVATING WORKERS

One of the two major themes of this book is that leaders must understand the context in which they are leading if they are to be effective. But it's possible for a leader to understand the context without knowing how to motive the team members in that context. If you can't motivate your team, you won't be effective no matter how well you may intellectually understand the context of your organization.

In this chapter, I describe a number of factors that can affect motivation that can apply in almost any context. Human nature being what it is, people generally respond well to the same kind of treatment no matter what the context. Perhaps surprisingly, I have found that most of what motivates workers are nonrational incentives, so I devote the greatest part of the chapter to discussing these motivators.

The Importance of Motivation

John Gardner, the author of several books on leadership, believes that the ability to motivate is the leader's most important attribute. He calls it "the heart of leadership." Effective leaders not only motivate people to act, but also build confidence in their subordinates and inspire them to become leaders themselves.

How, then, should leaders motivate their constituents? Traditional incentives such as pay and promotion are effective, but I think people work best when they really believe in what they are doing and feel part of what is going on. Studies conducted by Harvard professor Elton Mayo more than 70 years ago at the Western Electric Hawthorne Works in Chicago found that the group of workers who were studied improved their productivity no matter how much the researchers varied their work conditions. Mayo and his team concluded that workers had needs and expectations that went beyond rational and economic incentives and that the workers were pleased that the researchers showed so much interest in them. They, in turn, wanted to please the researchers. The results have become known by the famous term the "Hawthorne Effect."

Today, when job movement is much more prevalent, people feel less connected with an organization because it can merge any day with another organization. Organizations are, in general, much bigger than they have been in the past. This causes a loss of identity and feelings of alienation among employees. It's more difficult, but still possible, to use nonrational incentives in such an environment, and the effort is worth it in terms of the objectives of the organization.

Motivate Individuals

Marcus Buckingham, who once headed the strengths management practice for The Gallup Organization, has written a great deal about motivating employees through nonrational rewards. In his recent book, *The One Thing You Need to Know...About Great Managing, Great Leading, and Sustained Individual Success*, Buckingham describes what he considers the key issue that every leader faces: identifying the unique traits of each employee and turning those traits into improved performance.

Speaking at a Wharton Leadership Conference in June 2005, Buckingham explained the notions of motivation he developed in his book. He said good managers (and leaders) differ from bad managers (and leaders) in one basic respect: bad managers play checkers, while good managers play chess. "The good manager knows that not all employees work in the same way," he said. "They know that if they are to achieve success, they must put their employees in a situation where they will be able to use their strengths. Great managers know that they don't have 10 salespeople working for them—they have 10 individuals working for them.... A great manager is brilliant at spotting the unique differences that separate each person and then capitalizing on them."[1]

Gen. P.X. Kelley, the former commandant of the U.S. Marine Corps and a member of the Joint Chiefs of Staff, tells about an experience he had that vividly illustrates the need for a leader to understand the individual concerns of every subordinate. When General Kelley was in Vietnam, one of the Marines under his charge had the reputation of being a troublemaker. Other officers had tried to correct the offender, but with little positive effect. Determined to understand the source of the Marine's problems, General Kelley called the young man aside one day and began to ask questions about his home and background. To his surprise, he learned that the young Marine had trained as a classical musician playing the violin.

Without saying anything to the Marine, General Kelley planned a surprise. He asked the officer responsible for ordering supplies to pick up a violin when he next flew out to get supplies for his unit. The officer was baffled, but orders are orders—and he did what he was told.

Soon after the violin arrived, General Kelley called the Marine into his office. He had placed the violin behind the door, so the Marine couldn't see it when he entered the room. "Son, how long has it been since you've played the violin," the general asked.

The Marine said it had been a very long time. General Kelly responded, "Then why don't you turn around, and play me a tune?"

The Marine looked behind him and saw the violin, and tears came to his eyes. As soon as the young man picked up the instrument, the general saw he was an experienced violinist. He played a melody for the general and it seemed as though his world had changed. That Marine went on to become one of the most popular young men in his unit, constantly in demand for his musical talent at gatherings and parties. He became a model of discipline and good conduct.

Understanding the wants and needs of individuals can be extended to groups of individuals in the hands of wise leaders who have intuition and empathy. They can use nonrational incentives to cause all sorts of positive behavior in groups that they would like to encourage. This can go all the way from inviting the employee of the month to have dinner with the president, to being recognized in the corporate magazine or winning awards of one sort or another.

At American Education Centers (AEC), a company we had acquired that I describe in Chapter 7, "The Entrepreneurial Organization: Sharing Your Vision with Others," where we had more than 1,000 people working in jobs ranging from faculty members to placement representatives to building maintenance supervisors, we had an annual event we called The President's Club. This was open to everyone in the organization, and we selected attendees on the basis of annual performance. In addition, six or eight executives of the company were always in attendance for the entire event. It was amazing for me to find out that some of these individuals in our schools had never been out of their state or on an airplane or on a cruise, where we held several of these conferences.

Each conference lasted about three days. We organized the group so that teams might be composed of an executive, a maintenance supervisor, a technical computer person, and others. We held contests among them, utilizing skits that related to the work that we did. They would stay up half the night working on these skits to get the prize, just as they would do a lot of hard extra work to be able to be selected to the President's Club event in the first place. The winners took home to the various schools videos of their trip, which, in turn, motivated many other people to try to be there the following year.

The motivation that the President's Club conferences produced and the related results were enormous compared to the cost in dollars and time of organizing them.

Build Confidence in the Future

Marcus Buckingham, at the Wharton conference I described previously, asserted that the main responsibility of a leader "is to rally people for a better future. If you are a leader, you better be unflinchingly, unfailingly optimistic. No matter how bleak his or her mood, nothing can undermine a leader's belief that things can get better, and must get better. I believe you either bring this to the table or you don't."

In addition to being optimistic, great leaders need a strong ego to motivate employees. "If you are going to lead, you better have a deep-seated belief that you should be at the helm, dragging everyone into that better future," Buckingham said. "Virtually nothing about a leader is humble. I'm not saying they are arrogant, but their claims are big." Buckingham believes that successful leaders find "universal truths" to rally their followers. These truths stem from the basic human needs, fears, and desires that unite all people, across all cultures.

One example of these truths is fear of the unknown. "We all share a fear of the unknown," Buckingham said. "The problem for the modern-day leader, of course, is that you traffic in the future. The best way to turn anxiety into confidence is this: Be clear. Clarity is the antidote to anxiety. If you do nothing else as a leader, be clear."

Buckingham described how former New York City Mayor Rudi Giuliani provided a good example of effective leadership through clarity. When Giuliani took office in 1993, he could have turned his attentions just about anywhere. America's largest city certainly had a slew of problems. But Giuliani set one specific, clear, and focused goal for his administration: He would reduce crime and improve quality of life for residents.

Then he laid out three simple ways he was going to start making that happen. He announced he would get rid of the windshield washers who pestered New York City drivers; clean subways of graffiti and then keep the vandals away; and make all cab drivers wear collared shirts. The issues were, on their surface, minor. But they were relevant to New York City's residents—his constituents. By setting three tangible goals and then achieving them, Giuliani was able to build trust among residents and respect among his workers. That trust carried over as he tackled larger challenges that would reduce the crime rate, and within a few years of his arrival, the FBI named New York the safest big city in America. "You can do a lot worse than pick just a few areas you want to take action on right now," Buckingham said.

Bring Workers into Planning

People need to feel that, in addition to what is going on, they are being listened to, that their job is important, and that decisions just don't get dumped on them without anyone explaining why. You need to make them part of the process of determining how their area moves forward. Thus it would be foolhardy for a board of directors to come up with a strategic plan for the organization. What the directors must do is to require management to come up with a strategic plan that they can approve. If management comes up with the plan, the managers are going to feel part of the process and committed to it and believe that it is "their plan," not the board's plan. This process shouldn't stop with top management; it should go all the way down the line.

Someone might object and say, "That could take a lot of time." If the process is well organized, the time it takes will be more than paid for in the quality of the plan that is realized by people who know what's going on at their level. They can come up with better ways to change things than someone peering down from the ivory tower of the executive office. Many times, down in the organization, people talk about a new decision that is absolutely wrong, that they believe was put together by some idiot in the executive office who didn't really understand what was going on. It happens all the time and it's debilitating to an organization. It fosters an "us versus them" attitude.

Communicate in Person

Communication is absolutely essential to all parts of the organization so that people feel that they know what is going on, what is going to happen, and, hopefully, that they have some input into their own destiny. Some leaders believe that this can be done solely by memo and the house organ. These are important means, but the leader also has to go out as much as possible and do this in person. The benefits of the leader spending a good amount of time out in the line organization interacting with people and listening to their thoughts are very significant. And the fact that the leader has taken the time to be there is critical to the people's morale.

Keep the Executive Office Lean

Today, in some organizations that are highly centralized, decision making gets moved more and more to the corporate offices. This is often a mistake when more and more decision making should be taking place in the divisions. The only real way to guard against this problem is to keep a lean executive office. As the CEO of Touche Ross, about every three years I made a 5% or 10% or 15% cut in the executive office staff. We didn't necessarily fire the people—we moved many back out to the field. In addition, we never, ever took on more space for executive office functions. I've known leaders who have moved the corporate offices from one city to the next primarily so that they could cut the executive office staff in half.

As a part of the impulse to augment the executive office, there is the tendency to overpay executive office people and underpay the line staff. If you look at those who are contributing to your revenues and profits, who are meeting the customers, who are in charge of developing the people, you will almost invariably come up with line managers. But often if you compare their pay to that of some in the executive office, it seems out of whack. To admit this is not to demean the executive office's functions or the functional organizations that are needed in today's Sarbanes-Oxley regulated world. But nothing can substitute for top leaders out in the field where the rubber meets the road getting the job done. It's a terrific motivator for people to have the feeling that they are out there where it is happening, that they are making most of the decisions based on firsthand knowledge, that there isn't some bureaucratic morass keeping them from moving ahead and getting the job done, and that they are being recognized for what they accomplish.

At AEC, after the first CEO we hired didn't work out, I hired Bill Brooks from National Education Corporation, where he headed the Spartan Aviation Training Division, to come and be the CEO. You might ask why he would leave a big organization and a very prestigious job and join a much smaller operation where he didn't have the staff and corporate resources that he had in his previous position. The answer was that he wanted to run his own show. He didn't want bureaucracy. Brooks was confident that he could do a better job making decisions from his vantage point rather than hearing them from some corporate officer.

The first time we met to go over the following year's budget, he submitted the budget and operating cash flow numbers. We looked through the plans and I asked, "What about your capital expenditure plan?"

Brooks replied, "I haven't put that together because I didn't know how you did that here."

I asked, "Well, how did you do it at NEC?"

"We submitted our plan early in the year for the next year's capital expenditures budget," he said. "We then got it back with some comments. We resubmitted it. We then had someone tell us we needed to cut it by 10% or 15%. We resubmitted it and then toward the end of the year they sent us what they thought our capital budget should be and we moved ahead."

I asked him what he had in mind next year for AEC. He pulled out a sheet of paper and went over various things. I asked him a couple of questions and made a suggestion or two because of facts we knew that he would need to know. We then went on to other issues.

At the end of the meeting he asked, "Now what do I need to put together to get my capital budget approved?"

I said, "We just did that."

"That's why I like working here," he said. Top people, the kind you want working for your organization, want to be in charge of their area. They want to take responsibility, they want to make decisions, and they want to be able to move ahead with some speed as opposed to waiting for approval from somewhere. This is a powerful motivator. A lean executive suite can help you achieve this.

Head Off Turf Battles

Instead of moving decision making to the operating units, people often are hampered by the turf consciousness that builds up in certain bureaucratic organizations including, in some cases, academic institutions. It's not a case of what is best for the organization; it is a matter of who has the right to make the decision.

When I was at Wharton, I had a small development group and the university had a large development group—and we were supposed to work together to raise money for both the business school and the university. The central development group was mainly trying to raise funds for the university as a whole, particularly areas such as the School of Arts and Sciences, where it was more difficult to get money from the alumni, rather than Wharton, which had a very rich alumni base, making it easier to raise money. This arrangement could often be frustrating, especially when the university's development group put up roadblocks preventing Wharton from seeing some of the school's alumni.

One time, I asked the head of central development to sit down and have a talk because there must be some things I didn't understand. I said, "I view the university development group, and you in particular, as someone who is here principally to help me and other deans like me do their job. In other words, even though you don't work directly for us, you should certainly look at us as your customers. And frankly, I don't think I am getting much service. In fact, all I am getting are impediments that prevent me from doing my job."

He looked at me and said, "I don't view you as my customer at all."

I replied, "I know that—and that seems to be the problem."

Eventually we worked out an accommodation that wasn't optimal but was better for both of us than a constant turf war.

That approach of saying that, in effect, we worked for him was a demotivator in doing my job, and if I had used the same mentality in dealing with others in my organization, I would have demotivated them too. How many executive offices look at the operating units as their customers?

Respect Dissent

Most leaders have a strong intuition that allows them to sense and cope with dissent. To what degree, however, should leaders be willing to respect and accept dissent within their organizations? On the surface, it might appear that dissent can potentially undermine leadership by challenging the leader's authority. That need not always be the case, though, according to recent research by Michael Roberto, author of *Why Great Leaders Don't Take Yes for an Answer*.[2]

Roberto argues in his book that one of the most serious dangers leaders face is that they allow themselves to be surrounded by yes men who agree with everything the leader says. When this happens, the leader gets isolated and doesn't hear bad news until it is too late. According to Roberto, strong leaders are not afraid to encourage dissent and debate—but they take care that these discussions are constructive. Dissent, discussions, and debate are crucial to achieving genuine consensus. "Powerful, popular, and highly successful leaders hear 'yes' much too often, or they simply hear nothing when people really mean 'no.' In those situations, organizations may not only make poor choices, but they may find that unethical choices remain unchallenged," he says.

Roberto believes that organizations pay a high price when dissent is absent and poor decisions go unchallenged. Citing examples such as the Columbia disaster in February 2003, when the space shuttle disintegrated while reentering earth's atmosphere, and the Bay of Pigs incident of 1961, when a band of Cuban exiles "invaded" Cuba with the support of the U.S. government. In both cases, there were dissenting voices that were not heeded. He says that the best ally that a leader can have is a strong team of skeptical colleagues who are not afraid to speak up to challenge a misguided or ill-thought-out course of action. Although this might lead to a certain amount of conflict, it is a small price to pay for avoiding a much greater disaster down the road.

"Conflict alone does not lead to better decisions," Roberto notes. "Leaders also need to build consensus in their organizations. Consensus...does not mean unanimity, widespread agreement on all facets of a decision, or complete approval by a majority of organization members. It does not mean that teams, rather than leaders, should make decisions. Consensus does mean that people have agreed to cooperate in the implementation of a decision. They have accepted the final choice, even though they may not be completely satisfied with it."[3]

Build Confidence in Your People

If you proceed in the manner that I have described previously, you will build confidence in your people. Confidence is something they must have. It's debilitating if they don't. A person who lacks confidence will be merely a cog in the machine who does whatever he or she is told and completely lacks initiative. You want people who can make appropriate decisions at their level and are not waiting to be told what to do in every case. As I have said before, *He can who thinks he can.* The value of having a team of people who are not afraid to take positions, who are not afraid to make appropriate decisions in their area, who have confidence that they are in a position to make the best decisions, is immeasurable. It's powerful. If you put that together with a positive, forward-thinking attitude, you've got a winning combination.

A loss of confidence in an individual or an organization is a sure way to produce underachievement. Nothing is more debilitating to an organization than people who are filled with pessimism, malcontents who have a lack of confidence in themselves and the organization. You need to bring out the ultimate human potential in the individuals in the organization, and that has to be done with motivation, praise, communication, high expectations, respect, and confidence overlaid with a good dose of realism. You never want to be a leader who hollers at your workers in front of other people, demeans them for making a mistake, or generally treats them as if they're an inferior cog in the wheel. I am opposed to coaches who yell at players after they make a mistake on the floor during the game. No matter how much such so-called "tough managers" believe that this approach gets their job done, it never produces the high results that a positive approach can. Remember that one of the most successful basketball coaches in the history of the college game was John Wooden of UCLA. He approached coaching as *teaching* his players, and he knew he could teach them more by patience and respect than by yelling at them. Yes, I know that Bobby Knight has won a lot of basketball games, but I wouldn't want to play on his team, and today your top employees have a lot of options in other organizations.

You can get much more out of people in praising them and giving them credit in supporting them than the reverse. How many CEOs have you heard say, "I don't have people who are willing to take responsibility, make decisions, and take risks." If they were to look in the mirror, they would probably see that they made the people that way. At minimum, as a leader you are responsible for not changing the environment to one that encourages people to act in ways you profess they should not.

If people can't do the job, you have to fire them. You have to look out for the total organization, and everybody has to be able to carry their weight. But while they are there, you need to get the most you can out of their potential, and that is much better achieved by high expectations and praise than constant criticism and harangue. People want to be an organization where the glass is half full, rather than half empty. They want to be in organizations where when the going gets tough, the tough get going. They want to be in an organization where that's not a problem, it's an opportunity.

Tie Pay to the Strategic Plan

After discussing nonrational incentives, I end with a very rational motivator: pay. It is a very important part of motivating workers. Today, pay and promotion are used more frequently to motivate employees than maintaining a secure long-term relationship with the company in which the employee feels a part of what's going on. However, pay has unfortunately become tied more and more to a percentage figure of profit in an organization. Profits are important, but they are only one element of myriad goals to be achieved in most strategic plans. And in the long term, the overall strategic goals are more important than short-term profits.

Although profits are not easy to measure, it's easy to use the P&L number people designate as profit as a metric to decide what bonus to pay people. However, a truly effective pay system and promotion system must be tied to the strategic plan of the organization and the strategic plans of the individual units. You may hear the cry, "How can we measure all these soft items such as developing people, introducing new products, putting in a new marketing program, reducing turnover?" Further complicating this metric is that few managers want to be measured on growth as a factor as important as profit. Yet growth of the enterprise is at least as important in the long run as profits. These things and other more macro items in the strategic plan can be measured. It's not easy, but it can be done.

An effective incentive pay system has to be tied to the overall strategic plan. If you give one person responsibility for the strategic plan and someone else responsibility for the pay system, and they are not connected, who do you think is going to win? Obviously, it will be the person with the pay system. It doesn't take people long to figure out how the organization decides how much to pay people and gravitate to a behavior necessary to meet the incentive. If the incentive is purely profit, you are going to find that a lot of other things—especially investments for long-term growth—will get shortchanged. And if you continually push hard enough on the profit button, you may even find that some of the numbers seem to get distorted in order to "make the plan."

Let me end this section on the topic of CEO pay, which many feel is a tremendous problem. I don't believe that the problem is in paying top leaders/CEOs whatever it takes to adequately reward them. The problems I see are in the number of CEOs who aren't doing a good job or are doing a very bad job and getting paid as if they were doing an outstanding job. Basically, if you have absolutely outstanding CEOs/leaders, you can't pay them too much; but for every one of those who are being paid a lofty amount, there is certainly more than one who is doing a mediocre or bad job who should be paid much less. This is extremely demotivating to the troops when they see their wages frozen and people being laid off because the company isn't making enough money, and yet the leader seems to be making an inordinate amount of money. Having said all that, I feel there are some CEOs who should try to hold their compensation down not because they don't deserve it but so that their action will provide a motivation and incentive to the troops who, for whatever reason, aren't doing as well comparatively as the CEO. There have been CEOs who have done this, and I believe it generally has been a positive force. It is very difficult, however, to do this in today's business world, where the magazines compare every CEO to everyone else and it's difficult to see your name down below a group of people you know are not doing as good a job as you are.

When I was at Touche Ross, every individual partner was listed in a book as to how much he or she made each year. By and large, the partners were happy until they got the book and saw how they were doing compared to others that they knew. Everyone wanted to be on the "first page" of the book, and as I remember in the early days, this included 25 people. I told our people to make the type smaller so that we could get 50 people on the first page, and I think this was a plus. On the other hand, on several occasions I suggested to the people who were deciding my salary that I did not want the number to be over $X because that would put too much of a gap between me and certain of the other top people in the firm, and that would be demotivating. From my standpoint, when, as I remember, I was making about $500,000, the real question was not whether I made $100,000 or $150,000 more, it was whether the 800 partners in the U.S. firm could take a look at the first page and the page they were on and compare it to my salary and say I think that seems about right. Believe me, that would not have been the case if I was making a lot more money than the rest of the people in the top levels of the partnership.

Retain the Best People

One of the most important benefits of motivating your workers is to retain your best people. Marcus Buckingham, in another book with co-author Curt Coffman, titled *First, Break All the Rules: What the World's Greatest Managers Do Differently*, argued that companies don't just compete to sell products and services; they also compete to hire the best employees in highly competitive markets. Although HR departments historically have focused on developing attractive pay packages to hire and retain their most talented employees, this may not be enough.

"Today, more than ever before, if a company is bleeding people, it is bleeding value," Buckingham and Coffman write. "Investors are frequently stunned by this discovery. They know that their current measuring sticks do a very poor job of capturing all sources of a company's value. For example, according to Baruch Lev, professor of finance and accounting at New York University's Stern School of Business, the assets and liabilities listed on a company's balance sheet account for only 60% of its real market value. And this inaccuracy is increasing."[4]

Buckingham and Coffman collected data from more than 80,000 managers in more than 400 companies. They found that the single biggest stumbling block to corporate success is bad management in a company's middle levels. Buckingham and Coffman say: "The manager was the critical player in building a strong workplace." Leaders of companies, according to Buckingham and Coffman, have overlooked how important the "manager" issue is in motivating employees. "Senior managers in companies are guilty of the same omission: They have failed to train staff to be effective managers, and they have failed to supervise managers' performance effectively. Companies are awash in information, performance metrics, and statistical analyses of products and markets. But, ask the authors, what is top management doing to capture information about the effectiveness of their managers and the impact the managers are having on their direct reports? Far too little," the review notes.

One reviewer of Buckingham and Coffman's book neatly summarized their argument: "A company can offer employees generous compensation, benefits, and wonderful perks such as health clubs and daycare centers, and still lose the best workers. What many otherwise excellent companies miss...is that one mediocre manager can wreak havoc in even the best organization and send the most talented employees running for the exits."[5]

So yes, motivation is the heart of leadership, and effective leaders not only motivate people to act but also build confidence in their subordinates and inspire them to become leaders themselves. Essentially every study has supported the fact that nonrational incentives are at least as important as, if not more important than, the traditional dollar pay. Even in this new day of people being devoted more to their marketability than company loyalty, nonrational motivators do work, just as top leaders/managers know how to get more accomplished by teams of people than those who are not adept at motivating. In our numbers-oriented approach to measuring results and recognizing people, you can lose sight of the great advantage you could have when a motivated organization enjoys what they are doing, believes in what they are doing, and are doing it in an environment of integrity and leadership, and in a culture that they enjoy working in.

Summary

- You need to motivate workers if they are to realize the organization's long-term strategic goals. The value of having a team of people who are not afraid to take positions, who are not afraid to make appropriate decisions in their area, who have confidence that they are in a position to make the best decisions, is immeasurable. It's powerful. If you put that together with a positive, forward-thinking attitude, you've got a winning combination.

- Understand the needs and goals of the individuals in the organization.

- Build confidence in the future of the organization.

- Bring workers into the planning process and make them a stockholder.

- Communicate in person to as many in the organization as possible.

- Keep the executive office lean.

- Recognize and head off turf battles.

- Respect dissent and listen to it carefully before making decisions.
- Build confidence in your people by positive rather than negative means.
- Tie pay to the strategic plan, not just the quarterly profit figure.
- You will retain more of your best people when you motivate them by nonrational as well as rational means.

Endnotes

1 "Good Managers Focus on Employees' Strengths, Not Weaknesses," *Knowledge@Wharton*, June 29, 2005.

2 Wharton School Publishing, June 2005.

3 *Why Great Leaders Don't Take Yes for an Answer*, Chapter One, Wharton School Publishing, 2005.

4 Chapter 1, "The Measuring Stick," p. 23.

5 "The High Price Companies Pay for Mediocre Managers," *Knowledge@Wharton*, March 1, 2000.

Chapter 11

PUTTING IT ALL TOGETHER

I began this book by describing the principles of leadership that I strongly believe that all leaders need to be guided by. Then in the context chapters I brought in those principles that have a special importance in each context—though I made it clear that all the principles operate in each context, but in different proportions.

In this last chapter, I come full-circle back to the principles and relate them to context in a more general way. Whereas in the context chapters I brought in selected principles, here I will restate the principles and then tell you more about how I think they relate to context.

The chapter ends with some final thoughts about leadership that I want to share with you.

Integrity

A leader at all times must embody a personal integrity, which is the foundation of leadership. Followers want to believe that their leader is unshakably fair in public and in private.

Truly, a leader's integrity is independent of context. There is no organizational context in which integrity plays a subsidiary role to the other principles of leadership. The leader's followers should be able to trust that the leader is not only of the highest integrity, but also truly interested in them and their aspirations.

The leader must be consistently fair in public and in private to convey an image, real and perceived, of integrity.

If I leave you with no other cardinal rule, it is this that you should never forget.

Execution

A leader applies basically the same principles of leadership regardless of context, but the style of execution is very different in different contexts. That is, execution in leadership is to a great extent about context.

Execution is a key to getting anything done. As the leader, you must be involved in execution and not delegate all the execution to others. They must understand that you put a high premium on execution and expect them to do the same. How you execute your leadership role will differ with different contexts. Leading in a top-down organization is vastly different from leading in an organization of peers. Remember that you will be judged on how well you execute your strategic goals, and that requires that you understand how things get done in the context of your organization. Larry Bossidy wrote a whole book about execution, and I heartily recommend that you read it. It is filled with the wisdom borne of experience in getting things done.

Opportunities Ready for Change

In normal times, a leader should make faster progress taking opportunities that are ready for change rather than trying to take on areas that the leader knows will be more resisted. Later these resistance areas could be more conducive to change.

Opportunities for change will arise in any and all contexts. This is particularly true of an organization in crisis. Your leadership style needs to become focused and concise during a crisis. Crises create a sense of urgency and make it possible to make changes that may be harder to implement than at other, so-called normal, times. Crisis creates unusual opportunities, including the fact that as you "go through the fire together," you find out whom you can count on among your team. In Chapter 5, "The Organization in Crisis: Turning Danger into Opportunity," we saw that Marsha Evans regarded crisis as an opportunity. When things are going well, it's difficult to manage change; but when things are falling apart, the situation cries out for change. Followers will understand this.

In Chapter 6, "When Organizations Change: Transforming the Culture," I told how you need to be constantly on the lookout for opportunities to move the process along. The point is to remain alert to opportunities and regard the change process as dynamic and constantly evolving.

In a Crisis, Stay a Step Ahead of Followers

In times of crisis, a leader must step out ahead of the followers and make the difficult decisions without consensus and at times even without adequate explanation in order to resolve the threat to the organization.

In any organizational context that is in a state of crisis, you must not hesitate to take command and make those difficult decisions that will turn the situation around. Your long-term goal may be to build consensus among the key players in the organization, but that may have to wait until you are confident that disaster has been averted.

Context can influence how you manage the transition toward a more collegial organization. Peers will expect to have an increasing role to play as soon as the immediate crisis has passed. So will professors in an academic context. In a top-down context, you should have more time to begin to delegate to others.

Release the Potential of Followers

A leader's ultimate goal is to release the human potential of the followers. This will benefit not only the followers but also the overall organization.

You can't do it all yourself no matter what context you are in. All of Chapter 10, "The Heart of Leadership: Motivating Workers," is about how to release workers' human potential. Most of the motivating factors are the same in most contexts, and I urge you to use Chapter 10 as your basic reference for getting the most out of your workers.

Foster Innovation

In today's global marketplace leaders need to foster innovation at all levels of the organization, and that means listening to workers and giving them ample latitude to experiment, make mistakes, and seek new products and services that will compete in a constantly changing competitive landscape.

Fostering innovation in a top-down context is generally more difficult than, for example, in an entrepreneurial organization. But fostering innovation can be difficult in almost any context. Workers may have many good ideas and bad ideas, but if you don't make it clear to them that you and the organization want to hear them, workers will keep their ideas to themselves. Hearing the good ideas means not punishing the bad ones. That holds true in any context.

Followers' Aspirations and the Strategic Plan

A leader mobilizes followers by finding out their goals, desires, wants, and needs, and makes them believe that the leader is truly trying to help them achieve these aspirations. At the same time, in order to achieve the goals of the organization, the leader must bridge the individual goals of the followers and the overall goals that are incorporated in, for example, a strategic plan.

To be successful, leaders need followers. People follow leaders who are able to discover their expressed and unexpressed goals and aspirations, and become convinced that the leader will be able to help attain them. The goals of followers can differ widely depending on the organizational context. Professors in an academic context are likely to have different aspirations and goals from those of workers in a fledgling entrepreneurial organization. The task, then, is to understand the goals of workers in your organizational context and then help them to achieve their objectives. You will not give up your own strategic goals or those of your organization. Instead, you will find a way to bridge the two. When your strategic goals and those of your constituents are joined, it helps bring about real change and the ultimate goals can be achieved.

Remember too that different people in the same organizational context can have different needs and wants, and therefore they must be approached in accordance with what will be most successful. You should not say, "We have a sales force," but rather, "We have 25 individual salespeople." People are different and they will respond differently to certain motivations and stimuli. This complicates the task of a leader regardless of context, but success depends on responding accordingly.

Good Judgment

A leader's most important and essential attribute is good judgment. This is innate and really can't be taught, although it can be matured with experience.

Good judgment is required in all contexts. Enough said.

Build Confidence

A leader must build confidence among the followers. Like teachers, a leader must communicate high expectations and then ensure that followers develop confidence that they can meet those expectations. They can who think they can.

There is no context that I know of in which it is not important for a leader to communicate a feeling of confidence to followers. You must be a can-do person who rallies the troops; is optimistic; and, with a good dose of realism, explains how the organization is going to meet its goals, be successful, and be the best at whatever it does. All followers in all contexts want to believe that their leader is confident of the future and can lead them to the promised land. The leader's glass is never half empty.

Rewards That Motivate Followers

A leader must give considerable thought and careful execution to the whole area of rational and intangible rewards in relation to motivation of followers. For example, it is critical to the execution of a strategic plan that the compensation system be tied to the plan and not exclusively to earnings per share or the budget.

Motivation should be a continuing process in any context. This can be done through any combination of rational compensation systems or promotion or special events such as president's conferences or recognition or praise or other rewards, and it should be a constant stimulus to the individuals. In a top-down context the financial rewards should reflect how well workers implement your strategic goals. In an organization of peers, or an entrepreneurial organization, many workers can be rewarded on the basis of their measurable individual performance.

But keep in mind the intangible rewards that can mean as much as compensation. Regardless of context, your followers should operate in an environment where they believe they are in as much control of their destiny as is possible under the circumstances. They should be involved in the overall decision-making process that affects their particular area. They should be allowed to make decisions that are necessary and relevant within their area. When this happens, they have a feeling of fulfillment since they are not only responsible but also have the authority to operate in their area.

Plan Ahead but Don't Get Ahead of Followers

A leader can't get too far out in front of the troops in leading without risking failure to achieve the leader's goals. A leader will always be ahead in thinking, but the group must be brought along so that members understand what is happening and why—or the leader may be faced with a disconnect between the leader's goals and those that the members are willing to accept.

Context can influence how much of your vision you should articulate to the organization. In a crisis you can tell your people about your vision of a better future, and that can be reassuring to them. Also, in a top-down organization you have considerable latitude in telling followers where you want to lead them. You are, after all, the leader, and they should understand that they are expected to follow your lead.

However, in peer organizations, charting a course too far into the future can be very threatening to the vested interests of partners. It is sometimes better to set short-term and reachable goals incrementally that lead to your ultimate vision. On the other hand, in Chapter 8, "The Academic Organization: Learning from the Wharton Experience," I found at the Wharton School that I could articulate a new vision that the professors—who share some of the same views as partners—saw was in their interests. In the final analysis, it will be up to you to judge how distant a vision you can articulate in your particular context. That's part of the principle of good judgment.

Communicate with Everyone

A leader must communicate the leader's goals to the entire organization— ideally in person, but at least in writing in his or her own words—since communication is crucial to an effective organization.

In any context, if you want to move the organization forward, you have to tell everyone where you are taking them. And the best way to do this is to do it as personally as possible. Speak to large meetings of workers. Use some of the new technologies of teleconferencing if you can't gather everyone in meetings. Send emails to everyone if teleconferencing doesn't reach everyone. And don't forget the company newsletter as another channel.

No matter what channel you use, you should avoid corporate clichés. In a top-down organization, or an organization in crisis, it is probably all right to take a commanding tone. In a peer, entrepreneurial, or academic context, it is better to come across as a caring leader who is looking out for the best interests of the rest.

A Symbol of Leadership

A leader serves as a symbol and is perceived by followers to be on a different plane from the rest of the organization. Thus, the leader is constrained in what behavior is appropriate and not appropriate. He or she can only go so far in being "one of the boys."

As a leader, you are the symbol of authority in the organization. This is true no matter what context you are working in. But your relationship with your followers will have subtle differences in different contexts. As a leader of peers, you cannot stand too far aloof from the others because they probably regard you as one of their own and would be insulted—and unresponsive—if you were to act as if you are on a significantly higher plane than they. This is also generally true in academic and entrepreneurial contexts.

However, in top-down organizations and those in a state of crisis, you are better advised to avoid great familiarity with followers or your ability to get things done may be compromised.

But the followers hold you to a higher standard and your behavior must reflect this.

Leadership Makes the Difference

Leadership is the main differentiator in performance in most environments. People think that formulas, slick marketing, being first, the latest management tool, programs such as Six Sigma, and so on are the key differentiators in an organization. These other areas matter, but leadership alone is the key differentiator between organizations that succeed and those that fail.

This last principle is basic to my view of leadership. In organizations that have been successful—especially those over long periods—I have observed that there were leaders at the top who made all the difference. An organization of good workers but with a poor leader is hobbled as it strives to implement a strategic plan. This is true regardless of context.

Final Thoughts on Leadership

I conclude the book with some observations about leadership that I want to leave you with.

Business Education

Today much of the training people receive in business relates to specific, specialized material. Although that is fine, we should spend more time thinking about leadership. Leaders need to be broad individuals who can see the "big picture." This means that no matter whether a business school offers a single course in leadership or has a full leadership program, the stress should be on broad preparation for leadership and not on narrow technical details. The best kinds of readings to assign are history and biography—especially biographies of great leaders, as well as leaders who failed. There is probably no better model for would-be leaders to learn from than leaders in the past, some of whom have succeeded spectacularly, and some of whom have failed spectacularly.

The Ultimate Pitfall: Hubris

Probably the greatest potential pitfall many leaders stumble into over a period is that their egos get in the way because everyone around them is telling them what a great job they are doing. This can often happen in a top-down environment, but it can happen anywhere, including academia, peer-type organizations, and just about any other form of organization. The followers want to please their leaders, and, therefore, many feel that complimenting and telling the leaders how great they are will benefit the followers. Leaders, on the other hand, are optimistic and like to think things are going well rather than not so well. Some of them do not really want to hear opposing views and this becomes apparent to their subordinates. After a time, these leaders tend to become insolated, begin talking much more than listening, and are really averse to ideas other than their own. And it finally comes to the point where they say too often, "Oh, we tried that three years ago and it didn't work." This can be deadly, and leaders who fall into this trap to the extreme are on their way down.

In the End, It's All About People

The next time you are told that it's all about hedges, derivatives, algorithms, and quant models, it's about getting an "edge" in the transaction, it's about quarterly earnings and buying in stock and piling on debt, it's about being a tough boss who takes all the credit for wins and blames the subordinates for losses—don't argue. Just smile, because you know it's all about people and achieving their maximum potential and the goals of the organization—and that's all about leadership. Why are you smiling? Because you know you are going to beat those short-term, ends-justify-the-means thinkers every time.

I wish you success in your own leadership quest—go forth and win.

CONTRIBUTOR BIOGRAPHIES

Gordon Bethune is the Chairman of Aloha Airgroup (parent of Aloha Airlines). Before joining Aloha, he headed Continental Airlines. Bethune joined Continental as president and chief operating officer in 1994. He became the CEO the same year and chairman of the board in 1996. Bethune was previously a vice-president at Boeing. He holds a bachelor's degree from Abilene Christian University in Dallas, Texas.

Larry Bossidy is the former CEO of Honeywell International. He was the Chairman and CEO of AlliedSignal between 1991 and 1999. He became the Chairman of Honeywell after the company merged with AlliedSignal in 1999. Bossidy retired in 2000. Before joining AlliedSignal, he was the CEO of GE Credit, which later became GE Capital. Bossidy is a graduate of Colgate University.

Virginia Clark is the director of external affairs of the Smithsonian Institution. Before she joined the Smithsonian Institution in 2002, she was vice-president for development and alumni relations at the University of Pennsylvania. Clark is a graduate of Boston University.

David M. Cote is the CEO and Chairman of Honeywell. He became the CEO of Honeywell in 2002 and Chairman of the Board that same year. Before joining Honeywell, Cote was Chairman and CEO of TRW. Cote had previously worked for GE Appliances as its CEO. Cote holds a bachelor's degree in business administration from the Whittemore School of Business and Economics at the University of New Hampshire.

John J. DiIulio, Jr., is a professor of political science at the University of Pennsylvania and a Jesuit leadership expert. He is also the director of the University's Robert A. Fox Leadership Program. During 2000–01, he was assistant to the President of the United States and first Director of the White House Office of Faith-Based and Community Initiatives. Previously DiIulio was a professor of politics and public affairs at Princeton University. He holds a Ph.D. degree from Harvard University.

Thomas Ehrlich co-directs the Carnegie Foundation's Political Engagement Project and the Project on Foundations and Education. From 1995 to 2000, he was a scholar at California State University and taught at San Francisco State University in community-service learning courses. He was formerly president of Indiana University, provost of the University of Pennsylvania, and dean of Stanford Law School. He graduated from Harvard and Harvard Law School.

Marsha (Marty) Evans is the former president and CEO of the American Red Cross. Before that, she headed the Girl Scouts of the USA, which she joined after a 29-year career with the U.S. Navy. Between 1993 and 1995, Evans led the Navy Recruiting Command and also served as chief of staff at the U.S. Naval Academy at Annapolis, Maryland. She retired as a Rear Admiral in 1998, one of the very few women to do so. Evans holds a bachelor's degree in law and diplomacy from Occidental College in Los Angeles.

Gen. P.X. Kelley is the former commandant of the U.S. Marine Corps. He has led the Marine Corps at various levels from platoon through division and was the youngest Marine to be pro-moted to the rank of General. In 1979, General Kelley was appointed by the U.S. President as the first Commander of the Rapid Deployment Joint Task Force, which became the U.S. Central Command. He has won several medals from the Department of Defense and the armed services. General Kelley holds a bachelor's degree in economics from Villanova University.

Yotaro (Tony) Kobayashi has been the Chairman of the Board of Fuji Xerox and is its chief corporate advisor. He joined Fuji Photo Film in 1958 and joined Fuji Xerox in 1963. Having become a member of the board of directors in 1968, Kobayashi became the company's president and CEO in 1978. He became chairman of Fuji Xerox in 1992 and chairman of the board in 1999. Kobayashi holds a bachelor's degree from Keio University in Japan and an MBA from the Wharton School of the University of Pennsylvania.

John R. (Jock) McKernan is Chairman of Education Management Corp. He is also the former governor of Maine, having held that office for two terms from 1987 to 1995. McKernan, who is married to U.S. Sen. Olympia Snowe, went to Dartmouth College and also attended the University of Maine School of Law.

David Reibstein is a professor of marketing at the Wharton School of the University of Pennsylvania. He was previously the vice-dean of the Wharton School's Graduate Division. A former Executive Director of the Marketing Science Institute, Reibstein has won several academic awards. He holds a bachelor's degree from the University of Kansas and a Ph.D. from Purdue University.

Uriel Reichman is the Founder of the Interdisciplinary Center (IDC) in Herzliya, Israel's first private, nonprofit academic institution. Before founding IDC, he was Professor and Dean of Tel Aviv University's Law School; Chairman of the "Constitution for Israel" movement; and Chairman of the Israeli Human Rights Committee of Israel's Bar Association, among many other public service roles. He holds a Ph.D. from the University of Chicago.

Gen. Eric K. Shinseki is the 34th Chief of Staff of the U.S. Army and also the first Asian American to head one of the U.S. armed services. He has served in various command and staff roles in the U.S. and other countries, including two combat tours in Vietnam. Gen. Shinseki has taught at the U.S. Military Academy's Department of English. He holds a bachelor's degree from the U.S. Military Academy and a master's degree in English literature from Duke University.

Michael Useem is a professor of management at the Wharton School of the University of Pennsylvania and Director of the school's Center for Leadership and Change Management. His research areas include leadership, corporate governance, and corporate change and restructuring, among others. Useem has won several teaching awards and authored several books. He holds a bachelor's degree from the University of Michigan and a Ph.D. from Harvard University.

Jacob Wallenberg is Chairman of the Board of Investor AB and vice-chairman of SEB (Skandinaviska Enskilda Banken). He is also a member of the board of the Nobel Foundation. Born in Stockholm in 1956, he was educated at the Wharton School of the University of Pennsylvania, where he earned a Bachelor of Science in Economics in 1980 and an MBA in 1981. Mr. Wallenberg attended the Royal Swedish Naval Academy and is an Officer in the Royal Swedish Naval Reserve.

Yoram (Jerry) Wind is a professor of marketing at the Wharton School of the University of Pennsylvania and Director of the school's SEI Center for Advanced Studies in Management. In addition, he is Academic Director of the Wharton Fellows Program. Wind has written more than 22 books and 250 research papers. He holds bachelor's and master's degrees from The Hebrew University in Jerusalem and a Ph.D. from Stanford University.

INDEX

W-X-Y-Z

ЩД Wharton School Publishing

In the face of accelerating turbulence and change, business leaders and policy makers need new ways of thinking to sustain performance and growth.

Wharton School Publishing offers a trusted source for stimulating ideas from thought leaders who provide new mental models to address changes in strategy, management, and finance. We seek out authors from diverse disciplines with a profound understanding of change and its implications. We offer books and tools that help executives respond to the challenge of change.

Every book and management tool we publish meets quality standards set by The Wharton School of the University of Pennsylvania. Each title is reviewed by the Wharton School Publishing Editorial Board before being given Wharton's seal of approval. This ensures that Wharton publications are timely, relevant, important, conceptually sound or empirically based, and implementable.

To fit our readers' learning preferences, Wharton publications are available in multiple formats, including books, audio, and electronic.

To find out more about our books and management tools, visit us at whartonsp.com and Wharton's executive education site, exceed.wharton.upenn.edu.

Wharton
UNIVERSITY of PENNSYLVANIA

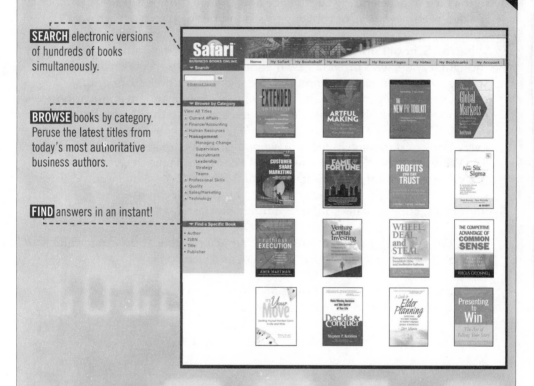